Crook and Chase

Crook and Chase

Our Lives, the Music, and the Stars

Lorianne Crook and Charlie Chase

with Mickey Herskowitz

William Morrow and Company, Inc.
New York

It is the policy of William Morrow and Company, Inc., and its imprints and affiliates, recognizing the importance of preserving what has been written, to print the books we publish on acid-free paper, and we exert our best efforts to that end.

Library of Congress Cataloging-in-Publication Data

Crook, Lorianne.
    Crook and Chase : our lives, the music, and the stars / by
Lorianne Crook and Charlie Chase.
        p. cm.
    ISBN 0–688–13128–X
    1. Crook, Lorianne.   2. Chase, Charlie.   3. Country
musicians—United States.   4. Country music—History and criticism.
I. Chase, Charlie.   II. Title.
ML385.C68   1995
781.642'092'273—dc20
    [B]   95–23411
                                                                                   CIP

Printed in the United States of America

First Edition

1   2   3   4   5   6   7   8   9   10

BOOK DESIGN BY RENATO STANISIC

To Mom and Dad, Uncle Floyd,
and my husband, Jim Owens.
Each of you in your
own way is responsible for everything
wonderful in my life.

To my wife, Karen, who knows me
better than anyone else and loves me anyway.

Acknowledgments

Much like a nightly television show, a book is often produced with the help of many unseen hands, keeping the lines open or untangled.

I, Charlie, would like to thank my wife, Karen, who did a great job as supporting author in reflecting, organizing, and relaying all the ups and downs of my life and career.

I, Lorianne, owe so much to my husband, Jim Owens, who is the mastermind behind the creation of the Crook and Chase team, and who gave country music, its stars and fans, what they always deserved, their own news and entertainment series on television.

The authors also owe a special thanks to Laurie Larson, our top gun in charge of traffic control, who kept the flight paths clear. Paul Bresnick, our editor, was a soothing and supportive presence and a welcome arbiter when ideas and deadlines clashed.

Our sincere thanks to Bill and Gloria Adler for believing in this book from the beginning.

And to Mickey Herskowitz, who had the courage and the talent to jump into the raging river of this book. Thanks for the rescue, Mick! You're a superhero to us.

And most certainly to the country music stars who have thrilled us and touched us in a million different ways. This book celebrates you.

Contents

Northern Exposure

A blustery rain pelted the sidewalks of New York, forcing us to seek shelter under a makeshift tent and the beach umbrellas down by the ice-skating rink in Rockefeller Center. The weather was more than a bad omen. Rain can delay your guests, interfere with the sound cues in your earpiece, and in general raise hell with a live, outdoor television show.

A large puddle of water had formed on the very spot where Martina McBride was to sing a cut from her latest album. The song had to be scratched, and we wondered if the legendary Tony Bennett would make it in for his appearance. Getting in from Long Island or Queens or anywhere in New York is no easy trick when the conditions are nasty.

Tony arrived on time and in a cheerful mood; he couldn't stop the rain but he made it seem a part of the backdrop. Our interview with Martina was lively. So were the ones with Harry Smith and Paula Zahn, the morning news team at CBS, and Jerry Orbach, the star of the TV series *Law and Order*. They all seemed genuinely excited and at ease appearing on the *Crook and Chase* show.

It was May 1993, and New York City laid out the welcome mat for the stars of country music and their fans. It turned into a huge campaign with a theme of Country Takes Manhattan. And country did. At least, you couldn't disprove it by the contingent that made the trip from Nashville.

We were in the seventh year of co-hosting our variety show on The Nashville Network. (By late fall we would expand into ninety minutes of prime time with a production called *Music City Tonight.*)

To cover the events, and to take part in them, we uprooted the *Crook and Chase* show and replanted it smack in the middle of Rockefeller Center. Our cameras were across the street from the General Electric building, and the offices of the National Broadcasting Company, which is where television was introduced to America in the 1930s.

Whatever your line—selling cutlery or high fashion, playing pro football, singing, dancing, acting, writing, or talking—you are eventually drawn to the Big Apple. It is, after all, the world's marketplace. These are the roots of show business, the home of Tin Pan Alley and Broadway and Carnegie Hall. You can barely turn around without hearing a high-fidelity sound track, if only in your head, of Frank Sinatra singing "New York, New York." As a first-time visitor or a frequent one, at some point you feel those little town blues. Then the second chorus kicks in with that timeless reminder, "If I can make it there, I'll make it anywhere."

Which brings us back to Tony Bennett, and how everything came together on a lovely, rainy, dreary evening in Manhattan. He had just released a new compact disc featuring his treatment of familiar Sinatra hits. And this is how the interview went.

LORIANNE: As I understand it, both Frank Sinatra and Bing Crosby called Tony Bennett the best singer they ever heard. I cannot think of a greater compliment than that.

CHARLIE: He wanted to pay tribute to Sinatra and the result is *Perfectly Frank,* the name of this new album (*holding up the disc for the camera*). What he did is take twenty-four of Sinatra's most popular torch and saloon songs and put them on this CD.

Lorianne then asked Tony if he thought he had done justice to Sinatra's songs, and he surprised us by saying no . . . but with an explanation.

TONY: I did it my way—no pun intended. I was just trying to prove something to the young entertainers, who are all writing their own songs, ever since the Beatles. Before that, a Sinatra or a Judy Garland, a Fred Astaire or a Gene Kelly, we were interpreters of the music. What I tried to show with this album is that if you're going to write, then stretch up to the great American composers like Jerome Kern and George Gershwin and Irving Berlin. They studied classical poetry. They made a craft of it.

CHARLIE: I think country music has some of the most talented song-writers to come along. They really know how to express their feelings.

TONY: That's what it's all about. If it's based on the truth, the music lasts.

LORIANNE: You have a connection to country music. You recorded "Cold, Cold Heart" by Hank Williams. Now, I understand Hank actually heard your version and was in awe of your arrangement. He thought it was absolutely beautiful.

TONY (*with a chuckle*): It's nice of you to say so, but that story isn't quite accurate. This is what happened. In those days, if you had a country hit you could count on selling about three hundred and fifty thousand records in the Bible Belt. It was quite consistent and they (the companies) made a lot of money. But my recording of "Cold, Cold Heart" was the first country record that sold internationally. It sold about two million copies around the world. I got a call one night from Hank Williams. We had never met. I called him Mr. Williams. He said, "Tony, what's the idea of ruining my song?"

CHARLIE: But he was just kidding around with you?

TONY: Oh yeah. He was joking. It was a sample of country humor.

CHARLIE: When you are singing, and I know people have noticed this, you have such a warm smile on your face. I don't think there is anyone who is happier singing than you are when you're onstage.

TONY: I learned that from Bing Crosby. When I was a kid I used to love to listen to Bing, and one of his secrets (of success) was that he just happened to enjoy singing. It had nothing to do with money. You put a song sheet in his hand and that was all he needed. I was very influenced by Bing Crosby and Louis Armstrong. Both of them just loved to perform.

CHARLIE: *Perfectly Frank* has been described as the ultimate fireplace album. Are you a true romantic?

TONY: Yes, I've always sung all kinds of love songs. I believe in love.

As we talked, sitting on high wooden chairs, we had to shift occasionally to avoid the rain that would build up and pour off the edges of the tarp spread above our heads. It rained all five days we were there. The elements didn't bother Tony Bennett at all.

LORIANNE: We were told that years ago you used to work not far from here, but not as a singer. Is that right?

TONY: When I was a young boy, going to art school, I worked on the third floor of the Associated Press. No one had ever heard the word "computer" back then. The stories came in on Western Union ticker tape, and I would carry the strings of tapes around to the reporters all day long.

LORIANNE: The whole time you were doing that, were you thinking about . . . wishing that you were a singer?

TONY: The things I loved to do were sing and paint. Everything else was just odds and ends. I did all kinds of jobs when I was a young boy.

CHARLIE: Do you keep up with all kinds of music—classical, jazz, rock, pop—or just what interests you?

TONY: I'm addicted to music. I don't do it just as a business. What I like are the virtuosos, like Hank Williams, like Billie Holiday, Fred Astaire, Louis Armstrong, Sinatra, Ella Fitzgerald. It's interesting to me to read about Vladimir Horowitz and Pablo Casals, Enrico Caruso and Luciano Pavarotti. I like the ones who made it way over the top, where you put them on the top shelf. They are separate and away from everybody else.

This is a man who was then touring with the Count Basie orchestra, who has been playing to sold-out auditoriums for forty years. You hear the humility in his voice when he talks of other singers, but his signature song, "I Left My Heart in San Francisco," is played around the world. Lorianne asked him if he could rate himself; was he at the summit? Did he rank as one of the classic artists? "I'm the greatest star I know," he said without missing a beat, and you knew that was a sample of New York humor.

Our reporters and cameras had scattered across the city to record the sights of Country Takes Manhattan. The festival had kicked off with Dolly Parton playing Carnegie Hall. Billy Ray Cyrus was the headliner at Radio City Music Hall, and at one point, he was literally halfway out his dressing room window, leading the fans outside in a sing-along. There were concerts in the park, and a parade of stars at Denim & Diamonds, the hot new country and western club just off Lexington Avenue. Wherever they appeared, Clint Black, Wynonna Judd, Marty Stuart, and Martina McBride packed them in. Others confirmed what we suspected even before we left Nashville.

Harry Belafonte: "New York is made up of more country folk than city folk."

Mary-Chapin Carpenter: "I know they love country music here and that isn't strange at all. Country music is what everyone wants to hear."

Larry Gatlin, starring on Broadway in *The Will Rogers Follies*: "These folks are hip. It's New York."

Lorianne pointed out that there were a lot of folks still not convinced that country music is really popular in New York City. But the most listened-to country radio station in America broadcasts right there, in Manhattan, WYNY. Marty Stuart paid a visit to the station and talked about how attitudes have changed.

MARTY: It's nice to see us coming in here like a herd. Country artists never got a lot of respect when they came up here to do TV shows, or whatever. It was like the Clampetts had come to town. Now there is a whole new respect for country music. Everywhere we go, we step off the bus and somebody is waiting to say hello. It's a nice feeling. But as someone said, if you don't do well here, you go home with your tail tucked between your legs and try again. New York is an adult-sized portion.

The trip to New York was important to us, and to our staff, because it reminded us of how much country music has changed. This was a point made in our interview with Martina McBride, who had her first hit with "The Time Has Come" and followed that one with "My Baby Loves Me Just the Way That I Am" and the smash single, "Independence Day." The country stars, like Martina, are serious about the sound and the messages in their music. They know country music reaches far beyond its southern stronghold into the hearts and lives of people everywhere.

LORIANNE: Country is growing and changing so quickly. How easy is it for you to figure out what to put on the album, what direction to take because of the changing winds?

MARTINA: One great thing about country music, especially now, is that we can all do our own thing. You don't really have to follow any path or trend. I just look for songs that I believe in and say what I want to say.

LORIANNE: When you do the town in New York, what do you do?

MARTINA: I shop.

Best of all, the visit to Manhattan reminded us of what was wonderful and unique about Nashville. This is where fantasy (Hollywood) and reality (New York) meet exactly halfway across the map.

LORIANNE: The first thing that comes to my mind is that Nashville is not what people expect. Many fans that Charlie and I come in contact with say they are surprised by two things. One is that very few people in Nashville dress "country." Most of us do not walk around town or go to restaurants in boots, hats, and jeans.

The other comment is that they can't believe how difficult it is to find country music stars performing in Nashville. You would think you could spend a vacation going to show after show, but you can't. Nashville is not a country concert town, certainly not like Branson, where a fan can see several major country stars every day. There are a few small but nice theaters cropping up. However, the only place you can consistently see live country music performed by major stars is on our show, on weeknights, and the Opry, on weekends.

This may sound strange, but country does not hit you in the face the minute you land in Nashville. I grew up in the suburbs, aware that country music existed, but not involved in it. My friends and I listened to pop and rock radio. The concerts we went to at Municipal Auditorium were to see Chicago, Bread, Olivia Newton-John, and the like. Even now, my thirteen-year old niece and her friends are into the rap artists who come to town. They almost never ask me for free tickets to *Music City Tonight!* Don't misunderstand. I believe that people in Nashville are very respectful of country music and the tourism it generates. But, in general, their lives do not revolve around it.

What I love about Nashville is that the city isn't stuck on one track and it doesn't stifle you. I'm living proof. I feel just as comfortable revisiting the campus of my alma mater, Vanderbilt University, as I do at a hoedown. It is not unusual for me to go hiking in the Tennessee hills in the morning, ride horses later in the day on a friend's farm, and in the evening attend the symphony or a touring Broadway play at the Tennessee Performing Arts Center. I can ride my motorcycle, looking not unlike one of the Hell's Angels, then hours later slip into a designer gown for a formal social function. The next morning, you can probably find my husband and me at a small country café eating grits and sliced tomatoes. Most places we know all the waitresses by name and they know ours. In short, it's tough to narrowly define Nashville . . . and that's the way we like it.

CHARLIE: Nashville is a big, progressive city with a small-town edge and caring people—in an old-fashioned way. When someone in your family passes away, neighbors bring a dinner over to you. They offer to take care of the dogs. Several years ago on Christmas Eve morning, a tornado hit the Brentwood area, about a mile from our house, and when we went there to help, our entire community had showed up, just to watch out for people's belongings.

If visitors come here with the same idea as they have for Hollywood, seeing the stars, they are likely to see them where they least expect—in the supermarket, the hardware store, driving down the road. It surprises people to learn that the music industry, although perhaps the most well known, is but one of several thriving industries in Nashville, including publishing, finance, and health care. The Thomas Nelson Company is the biggest publisher of Bibles in the world.

The Civil War was fought all around this area. There are markers everywhere, indicating big battles—not skirmishes—where thousands were killed. A lot of the plantation homes, which still stand, served as hospitals. Some of them have bullet holes from the Civil War and the owners keep them that way.

My attorney bought an old house just outside Nashville in Murfrees- boro to convert into an office, and they found a skeleton under the house, with part of his sword at his side. There are people in town who think his ghost still haunts that house.

Very diverse people live here. There is an annual event called the Steeplechase, held at Percy-Warner Park, a hundred years old. You see at one end of the field the upper echelon of society in their riding attire and turn-of-the-century dress. At the other end, you see people in cutoffs and tank tops, sitting around tubs of beer, watching these very valuable horses perform. Princess Anne was a guest one year, but I don't think she was with the tub-of-beer crowd.

You think of Andrew Jackson and Opryland, but if you go out to the west end you will find an exact replica of the Parthenon of Greece. It was part of an exposition built in 1896. Although it was originally designed as a temporary structure for this celebration, the government came up with a project to restore and preserve it in the 1920s. Now the one in Greece is falling apart and our replica is in its original condition. Nashville has been called the Athens of the south.

Geography had a lot to do with Nashville becoming the capital of country music. We are right in the center of where much music was born. In east Tennessee, the Carter Family was going strong around 1930. From Kentucky, Bill Monroe spread his bluegrass music across the Ozarks, and the blues were born way down south. They came together in the wagon wheel that is Nashville. We're the heart of Middle America.

Country music continues to change. Yet in many good ways it remains the same, mainly because the people who write and sing the songs respect tradition as they break new ground.

We have the same respect for that tradition, yet we are pleased to have guests such as Tony Bennett, Kirk Douglas, Lily Tomlin, and Rush Limbaugh, because this is how we—and our audience—display our diversity. This is our world, and welcome to it.

The Cheerleader Who Spoke Russian

The turning point in my life probably came when I decided not to spy on the Russians for the Central Intelligence Agency. Unless you know me, that sounds like a joke. But it's true. I have studied foreign languages since my teens, and seriously considered taking a job with the CIA. So, what's a girl who speaks Russian doing in country music? The answer to that proves that no matter what you think you've prepared yourself for, you never know where life is going to lead you.

I was twenty-two when the CIA interviewed me, probably the first extraordinary thing to happen to me. But I'm getting ahead of myself. I had navigated my way into young adulthood, through years so normal and stable I probably should worry about what I must have missed. If my childhood lacked anything, it was trauma and adversity.

And yet I certainly had the potential to be a difficult child. I almost didn't make it into this world on February 19, 1957, in Wichita, Kansas. Mom had experienced an easy birth two years earlier with my sister, Kim. So feeling very confident in the last months of her pregnancy with me, she kept up her usual pace: darting all over the house, painting the walls, running up and down the basement stairs to do the laundry. She always had boundless energy.

When Mom complained of some slight cramping and bleeding, her doctor recognized the symptoms as early signs of possible miscarriage. He warned her to slow down immediately. Mom told me she was so uncomfortable she was in tears the last few weeks. It wasn't that I was big, just active. Many nights she couldn't sleep because my kicks were so strong and frequent. In fact, at her last prenatal exam, the doctor told her to expect a "little football player."

Mom and Dad decided to name me Derrick. Surprise! They didn't even have a girl's name picked out because they were so sure I was going to be the linebacker the doctor had predicted. Their first impulse was to name me Roxanne and call me Roxy for short. Then Mom started worrying that it would make me sound like a stripper. Instead, she got creative and combined two of her favorite names into Lorianne, and gave me a French middle name, Lynée—which I've been told means "little flower."

Fragile I was not. Before I was two, I had developed a fascination with my father's toolbox. According to family legend, they wondered why the dining room table was so wobbly until they discovered that I had crawled underneath and begun playing with Daddy's screwdriver. I had figured out how to loosen the screws.

They had to keep a constant eye on me. I was your basic tomboy, rushing to meet every moment of life. I loved to swing dangerously high on the swing set. I climbed trees and went swimming in the ditch in our backyard after a heavy rain. I remember thinking that mud was a wonderful thing.

Once, when I was still a toddler, a concerned neighbor telephoned Mom and said, "Are you aware that Lorianne is in your backyard, all by herself, climbing up the slide and sliding down as fast as she can?" Mom assured her that I wouldn't fall, and that she was indeed watching me from her kitchen window.

I was blessed to have two parents who were free, generous, and loving, and not frightened by these early signs of an independent nature. They allowed me to explore my physical and mental limits. Looking back, I think it was kind of like the army recruiting slogan: Be all that you can be.

In fact, Mom was upset when my kindergarten teacher predicted that I would be the "social butterfly" of the family. Mom and Dad were much more interested in developing my brain than my social status. They always made sure that any socializing was balanced with education.

Mom grew up in a time and place when she saw too many women whose husbands left them with kids, who had no means of support and no job skills. She and Dad were determined that their girls would be educated and able to take care of themselves.

It was no accident that I became so serious about my studies. My mother has a master's degree in elementary education and was once named Teacher of the Year for the state of Tennessee. She has a rare capacity to take on tremendous amounts of work and responsibility, and could organize an army if she had to. Mom is a true matriarch, the one we all turn to in our hour of need or time of trouble. She also happens to be an excellent shopping buddy!

Dad is an analytical chemist, a really brilliant man in many ways. He speaks German, loves the opera, is a terrific tennis player, and used to drive Mom daffy taking appliances apart and putting them back together. If the coffeepot was broken, he would dismantle it to find out the problem. Nobody had any coffee until he put all the pieces back. In recent years, he's suffered from a baffling ailment, called chronic fatigue syndrome, for which there is no cure, so he can't always do all the strenuous things he enjoyed. But I always see in him the quiet strength that certain men never have to demonstrate. You just know it is there.

Dad was always smooth about discipline. I remember riding a bicycle near the tennis courts when I was a second grader, and scaring my mother out of her wits. I would take my feet off the pedals, put all my weight on the handle bars, and zoom down a hill holding on with just my arms. Mom was certain I would be maimed or killed. Very calmly, Dad left the tennis court and walked over to me. "Do you realize," he said, "that what you are doing is dangerous and it could hurt you?" I said that I did. "Well, then," he replied, "it's your choice. You can continue to do that and I'll tell your mother that you are willing to take the risk. Or you can choose to make the smart decision and stop riding that way. It's your decision."

He didn't order me to do what he wanted me to do. He didn't lose his temper and take my bike away. So there I stood, a second grader thinking "It's my choice. I can make this decision for myself."

At that moment, my parents gave me a precious gift. I grew up knowing that everything was a choice, and that the consequences would be my problem or my success. I remember that incident as clearly as if it happened yesterday. It was a lesson that stuck with me: Everything in life is a choice.

Ours was not a life of wealth or privilege. We were a two-income family and had what we needed, few luxuries and no hardships. I don't want to paint us as a TV sitcom, but Mom was funny and cute in a classic 1950s way. She was like June Cleaver in *Leave It to Beaver*. She dressed up each morning in a matching outfit and high heels. She would cook breakfast and vacuum the house in her matching suits. She had postponed college to have three children—my brother, Bret, came along two years after me. When we were old enough to care for ourselves, we watched her go back to school and get her teaching degree. I have been around a lot of self-sufficient people.

Mom and Dad were considered some of the coolest parents in the neighborhood. I was proud of that. They were fun—but always wise in how they dealt with us. Both smoked at one time. They did not keep liquor in the house, but would have a glass of wine or champagne now and then. One New Year's Eve, Mom was having a cigarette and we noticed a bottle of champagne. She sensed that this was interesting to us. She said, "Kids, if you're ever curious about anything like smoking or drinking, adult things that you think might be fun, don't go out in the street and do it with your friends. Come talk to us. If you want to try a cigarette, you can try one here."

I sat on the couch that New Year's Eve, twelve years old, with my first cigarette and a small glass of champagne. Mom and Dad wanted us to know that we were perfectly free to express our curiosity, but it was not okay to sneak around and experiment behind their backs. The cigarette smoke gave me a headache and the champagne tasted like battery acid. The mystery was gone, the sneaky-fun feeling was gone. I don't recall ever taking a puff off another cigarette since that night. I never had an interest in trying it again.

As a result of their attitude I had no desire to try drugs. I grew up in the sixties and seventies when the drug culture was going strong, but I have never smoked a joint. Some of my boyfriends smoked pot, but I wouldn't let them do it around me. Maybe I came off as a Goody Two-Shoes, or holier than thou. But I wouldn't stay in a room with people who were doing dope. I'm sure they thought I was backward, but nobody ever said anything. All I know is, my sister, brother, and I made it through the hippie era. They grew up to be terrific people and I love to brag about them.

Kim has a master's degree in psychology, and has always been a real intellectual. She speaks German and Italian, studies poetry, and reads books on philosophy whose *titles* I don't even understand. Her husband, Ted, is a pediatrician in the army. They have three exhaustingly bright and exuberant children, Teddy, Danny, and Ashley, ten, eight, and six. Along with Kim, they are close to earning their black belts in tae kwon do. They can split boards with their bare feet. When the kids ask me for spending money, how can I say no?

Bret is the free spirit of the family. College was not his thing, but he has a way of plunging into whatever interests him. He can build anything with his hands, repair cars and boats, tend bar; he speaks Spanish, has a talent for photography, plays the guitar, writes songs and poetry, is big on camping and white water rafting, and is a terrific cook. You know the type: The person most likely to survive if stranded on a desert island. I have never met anyone who didn't like Bret. He has a heart as big as Texas. Though divorced, he and his ex-wife, Cathy, are on good terms. They gave me my first niece, Jana, who is charming and smart and currently addicted to roller skating. Funny thing, so was I at age twelve.

Another important person in our lives was my dad's brother, Uncle Floyd. When we were preschoolers in Wichita, Uncle Floyd would take us to pancake breakfasts on Sunday mornings. We dragged him to the five-and-dime and he bought us any little trinket our hearts desired. A bachelor, he lavished his time, attention, and money on us. Our affection for him was certainly not based on superficial things. The people in life you can count on, who truly matter, are few, and for our family Uncle Floyd was one of them.

Mom has always said that she and Dad would not be where they are today without him. He loaned them money to help build a new home and even to pay some of their maternity bills. He baby-sat for all of us so Mom and Dad could get their college degrees.

Uncle Floyd lived with my husband and me, enriching us with the pleasure of his company and his humor. Until recently, for seven years, he helped take care of the house and the grounds. In early 1994, he underwent surgery to remove a malignant brain tumor. The follow-up radiation therapy left him weak and in discomfort. But when I was home with a bad cold, he still insisted on bringing me a cup of herbal tea when he heard me cough. That is a perfect example of how unselfish and caring he was. Uncle Floyd died at our home on June 29, 1995.

Surrounded by these wonderful people, my growing up was not a difficult time for me. I don't think we kids were spoiled or indulged and I didn't have a fantasy childhood. But it is rich with sweet memories. I grew up without fear and plenty of space, and moved easily—or so it seems now—from one stage to the next.

When I was five years old, Dad moved us from Kansas to the lush, rolling hills of Tennessee, and I reveled in it. I was always running and climbing and jumping. I would tear around the yard on my bicycle, pretending that I was in the popular TV show *Rawhide,* screaming at the top of my lungs, "Head 'em up, move 'em out." I took part in the touch football games in our neighborhood until I realized that the guys were grabbing me in places that had nothing to do with football.

My grandfather built a tree house in our backyard on a tree with a thick vine. I swung on that vine until it finally broke. That was typical of me. I liked anything physical. I was on the school gymnastics team and I loved to dance. In high school, I was a cheerleader and homecoming queen, but not the babe of the school. There were always two or three other girls who were the babes.

I was studious to the point of being a bookworm. If a teacher said she wanted a three-page report the next day, I turned in five pages. If you were supposed to read ten books over the summer, I read twenty. I can't explain why, but I had a need to do more than was expected.

In junior high, boys were important. I started dating, but it was different from what goes on today. Back then in our crowd, nobody could afford cars.

"Dating" meant a boy coming over to the house, sitting on the front porch or back porch, and walking in the yard. Once I started dating someone, I stayed with him for two or three years. I was serious about relationships, even then. I didn't have a boyfriend just because he was captain of the football team. I had my own criteria: I dated a boy for his personality, because we got along and had fun. I didn't care what anybody else thought of him. If we could be close and confide in each other and do things together, then to me that was a boyfriend. I had only two or three relationships from junior high all the way through college, and, to be honest, I was much too busy with other things to center my life on boyfriends.

If there were report cards, I wanted straight A's. If there were clubs, I joined them—including the Beta and the Russian clubs. I worked as a waitress, at sixteen, and continued through college. It wasn't a job I liked much, but the money helped pay my way.

I had an odd advantage over other girls my age. I didn't care what my peers thought of me. I tried to please my parents and my teachers. This had the curious effect of inspiring not jealousy, or envy, but a kind of respect. I walked into a classroom and pretty soon I was the chairman of a committee. I was shocked one day when my English teacher told me I had been picked as editor of the school newspaper. What? I didn't even want to *write* for the paper. Now they were telling me the whole paper was my responsibility. But the faculty had made the decision and I actually enjoyed it, especially since they let my friends and me do "commercials" for the coming edition over the PA system.

My parents barely saw me when I was in high school. As class president, and captain of the cheerleaders, I planned pep rallies, school dances, fundraisers, and the prom. I didn't hang out in parking lots, drink, or do drugs simply because I knew it was wrong. To me, those things had "dead end" written all over them. I wasn't just trying to claim the moral high ground. I refused to misuse my time.

Once, I was a passenger in a car when the other girls decided to steal street signs. It was just a prank, but it was against the law and a silly, senseless thing to do. I just sat there, stuck in the back seat, not speaking to anybody. When the car stopped, I jumped out and walked home. I was sixteen and thinking, "This is no fun. This is destructive. I'm leaving." I didn't care what they thought, or if anyone teased or snubbed me the next day (no one did).

During my senior year, the principal, Mr. James Curry, called me into his office. There were just a couple of weeks left until graduation and I thought I might be in some kind of trouble. Nervously, I sat in front of his desk and waited. "In all my years," he said, "I've never seen a student like you. You have been an outstanding leader for this school and we're going to miss you." I was speechless. Then I burst into tears. It was the biggest compliment of my seventeen-year-old life. At that moment, I did a bit of growing up because I realized that what you do, and how well you do it, does have an impact on the people around you. At graduation, I was awarded the Faculty Medal of Honor, a huge Olympic-looking medal. It is still one of my prized possessions.

I went through college at the same fever pitch. Having accepted a scholarship to Vanderbilt University, I didn't want to blow it. I didn't join a sorority, didn't go to parties. Perhaps I was boring, but I graduated magna cum laude six months early, antsy to get out into the world. But fate had already played its hand in my life and I didn't even know it.

During my last year of college, I tried to put aside some extra money. In addition to waitressing, I had taken a job at Nashville's new baseball park, Greer Stadium. I was a Soundette for the Nashville Sounds, the Cincinnati Reds' farm club in the Southern Association.

There were about a dozen of us who wore shorts and halter tops, and our main job was to be friendly and helpful to the fans and sell programs. We also swept the bases between innings and took Cokes to the umpires, that sort of thing. As my luck would have it, the team's general manager, Larry Schmittou, decided to have the Soundettes tape a string of commercials to promote the games. And that was how I got into television. Channel 2 News in Nashville did the commercials, and some of the crew members began to mention that I had a certain ease on camera. They asked me if I'd thought about being in television. Of course, I had not.

At the time, my goal was to be an interpreter in the diplomatic service. I had earned my degree in Russian and Chinese and had studied political science and world history. But, at twenty-one, I didn't have a clue as to how demanding that kind of government job could be. The career seemed adventurous and romantic. I imagined myself traveling the globe and being involved in events that changed the world. Looking back, I don't think I would have been nearly tough enough.

Once it had been suggested, the idea of a television career intrigued me. After I graduated, I made the rounds of all the Nashville stations asking for a job. The only encouragement I received was from Channel 2. The news director, Lee Bailey, said, "You're green as a gourd, and we can't hire you, but we could take you as an intern if you were still in school."

Well . . . I had already graduated, so I devised a plan. I went to Nashville Tech and signed up for classes in typing and shorthand, figuring I would use those skills as a reporter. Then I went back to Channel 2 and said, "I'm a student again, so can I be an intern?" Bless Lee Bailey. He rolled his eyes and laughed and said yes!

Interns didn't get paid because you were there to learn. So I worked for about a year for nothing. I worked a full schedule, even holidays. I rode with reporters in the news cars, wrote copy for the newscasts, and even assisted the reporters in writing some of their stories.

My first thrilling TV news experience happened during my internship. I jumped in the news car to tag along on yet another story, and on the way the reporter told me that he was putting the ball in my court. *I* would be covering the story and *he* would watch! This was also the first time I realized that news reporters didn't take too kindly to covering entertainment. They called it "fluff," and it was beneath them. For me, nothing could have been meatier. I should have been petrified because of my inexperience, but I remember feeling nothing but exhilaration. Stella Parton and her sister Freda were making an announcement about a joint project. I walked right in, waited till the cameraman told me he was rolling, and went at it. The interview was short and to the point, but there were lots of laughs. I couldn't believe I felt so comfortable. We shot some extra footage and headed straight back to the station, where I put together a short piece, less than a minute, which made it on to the 10 o'clock news. Anne Holt was, and still is, a long-standing and highly respected anchorwoman in Nashville. When my words came rolling out of her mouth it was a moment of Olympic proportions for me. I felt like doing the Rocky dance that Sly Stallone made so famous in his first movie. My old buddy Lee Bailey, the news director, told me that if he were grading me on that piece I would only get a C, but all that mattered to me at that moment was that my work had made it on to live television and was delivered to perfection by Anne—by God—Holt!

By now I was torn about which career to pursue. I couldn't decide if I wanted to work for the government or stay in television. So I set up a meeting with a CIA recruiter, an experience I will never forget. We met at a LaQuinta Motor Hotel in Arlington, Texas. During the interview, he briefed me lightly on what a CIA agent does and gave me some materials to read. We conversed in Russian a bit so he could judge my level of competence. Thinking back on it, I must admit that the situation was scary to me. I was only twenty-two. For the most part he just sat there and stared at me. "You're such a little flower," he said, "nobody would suspect you of being an agent." To him that was a plus. It struck me as strangely ironic that he called me a "little flower," since that is supposedly the meaning of my middle name.

It wasn't the kind of meeting you might expect, based on our impressions from the movies. He didn't check out the salt shaker, cast furtive glances over his shoulder, or speak into his lapel pin. But, yes, it was a little spooky.

He told me, "You could be on the Chinese border for months living in a tent and you wouldn't be able to tell your family where you were or what you were doing." He added that I wouldn't be able to have the kind of close relationships I have now. I walked out of there realizing how little I understood about the CIA, and that was probably more than I wanted to know.

After that, I never looked back. I made the decision to stay in television and I progressed quickly. It all seemed so natural, as if this was where I was meant to be. Television news is very infectious. Nearly everybody gets a kick out of being on television—check out otherwise normal people mugging for the cameras and saying "Hi, Mom." But I enjoyed getting the story, being out in the news car, talking to people, finding out what had happened.

The usual path into TV news was from radio or print. It was rare for anyone to break in fresh from the campus. I was fortunate. I didn't have to struggle in one place, year after year, and try to get noticed. However, I knew my early work was embarrassing (but not for long). A news director or another reporter would say, "What you've done isn't airable, but you have some potential. If you work hard, you can be good." So I always had support and I improved quickly.

In those earlier years, when I was an intern at Channel 2, some people said I had to be crazy to work without getting paid. But I felt I was doing something important and I thrived because I was learning so much. Technically, I wasn't even an employee, but I typed on the computers and I ripped copy and handled all the camera equipment. I did as much as they would let me do because it was thrilling. The union filed a grievance against me because I wasn't a member or even a real employee; and I drove the station personnel nutty at times because I was trying to soak up as much information as I could every day.

I could not have survived without the support of my parents back when I was working for free. I was living in their home so I didn't have to pay any rent. I was eating their food and driving their car. They believed I was onto something, and dedicated to it, so they never said a negative word.

While I was at Channel 2, I got involved with a photographer and when he moved to Dallas I moved too. I took a job as a waitress again, working nights. I rented a typewriter and during the day I typed up résumés. I mailed them to sixty stations across the country and got two responses, both from Texas. One was a rejection from El Paso, and the other was from KAUZ-TV, Wichita Falls, with a note that said "If you're ever in the area give us a call."

So the first thing I did was save enough money to hop a plane to Wichita Falls. As it turned out, the very day my résumé landed on the desk of the news director, Lynn Walker, a reporter had walked out. He had a pile of them, and he picked up mine first because it was the most recent to arrive. He saw the Vanderbilt seal on my résumé and noticed that I spoke Russian and Chinese. He tossed it to the assignment editor and said, "Call her. If she can speak Russian, she can do news in Wichita Falls. Call her and see if she'll come."

And I did. I auditioned and got hired in the same day. I was barely twenty-three and just out of school. I stayed a year. I was a reporter for maybe six months when the female host of the *PM Magazine* show took a hike. She just quit. The station management was frantic. *PM Magazine* was a national chain, but the station had to have a local host. The station manager called me in and said, "We need somebody fast. Of all the people at the station, we think you can do it."

I was given a big raise—from $9,000 a year to $14,000. At the time, I thought I was rich. The timing was perfect for me because I had concluded that hard news reporting was not my calling. I had just gone out to report on the trial of a mother who had cut out the heart of her infant after she had seen a movie that portrayed a similar scene. The jurors were looking at photos of this mutilated baby and I thought "I can't do this." I was coming to the realization that I didn't have the heart, or the stomach, for the gory side of the news.

PM Magazine was more my style. It was a thirty-minute nightly show, Monday through Friday, with all kinds of features. It aired in about one hundred cities. Mostly it was light news and feature-type reporting. Every now and then it would offer something of a more serious nature, like a medical breakthrough, but mostly it was interviewing colorful people. Each city had its own hosts, male and female. My co-host was Michael James.

Through this period of time, I had never really thought about the next step. Things just unfolded on their own. I knew I had a personality that people enjoyed watching, at least, in this little town in Texas. Getting good information out of people I interviewed came easily to me. They seemed to feel comfortable with me, and I felt comfortable asking them all kinds of questions. I started to think I had some sort of knack for television.

After about six months on the job, I heard the *PM Magazine* franchise in Nashville was looking for a female co-host. I had never dreamed I would be good enough to work in a larger city like Nashville so quickly, but that didn't keep me from calling to ask about applying for the co-host position.

I was told that they finished their auditioning and were down to the wire. I told the executive producer, Judy Cairo, that I had grown up in Nashville and would be a good reporter for the city. Would she please consider me? Finally, Judy agreed and I quickly sent off a tape. She called back in the next couple of days and asked if I could fly in for an audition. On the set, I was teamed with the male co-host they had already picked, Jon Burnett, who is now a very popular TV personality on KDKA in Pittsburgh. Unbeknownst to me, the camera was rolling while Jon and I were figuring out what we wanted to talk about and who would say what.

The producers wanted to see if I was easy to work with, if I had ideas and was creative. They were watching every move and I didn't know it. I felt good about the audition. Judy called me at my mom's house that night and asked if she could meet me before my flight the next day, in the airport restaurant.

She made me an offer on the spot of $25,000. I thought "My God, I'm going to be even richer." I flew back to Texas and did about two more weeks of *PM Magazine* in Wichita Falls. Again, the timing was almost uncanny. After I left, the management decided they would drop the show. It was a small town and it was expensive to own the *PM* franchise.

I was twenty-four and on my way back to Nashville. I was going to be hosting a television show in my hometown and making $25,000 a year. That was pretty heady stuff.

As the co-host of *PM Magazine* for most of the next two years, I did entertainment interviews with the likes of Michael Martin Murphy and the Oak Ridge Boys. At the time, country music stars were largely ignored by the Nashville media. I was surprised by how much the artists seemed to appreciate doing an interview that would give them national exposure. I developed a real rapport with them.

At the same time, I started doing medical and health specials for Channel 2 that won some national awards. Then I did a story for *PM Magazine* about an amazing sixteen-year-old boy who worked in a gas station to earn spending money. One night he was robbed and stabbed twenty times in his head, face, shoulders, and chest. Not only did he live to tell about it, he battled back to become a functioning human being. I won the American Women in Radio Television Reporter of the Year award for that story.

It really began to sink in how big an impact I could have on people through my work. I also did some funny pieces that prompted letters saying "I laughed all night long" and "I had a hard day at work and you really made me laugh again." I was reaching people in ways I had never imagined. A TV piece that I put together could make others laugh or cry; it was a heavy feeling, but a satisfying one.

I owe so much to my first two co-hosts, Michael James and Jon Burnett. They were my best buddies, and they taught me invaluable lessons about teamwork, good work, and hard work. I was a rookie, but they never treated me like one. They gave me great memories of learning and of laughter. I am forever grateful for their kindness and patience.

When I was twenty-five, I got a call from my executive producer, Judy Cairo, who had been talking to a television producer named Jim Owens. He was producing an awards show with huge stars like Willie Nelson and Kris Kristofferson. She told me it was an important show and that Owens had specifically asked for me to cover it. The assignment was big for me because I would get to interview George Jones.

What I didn't know at the time was that Jim had seen my picture on a billboard while he was driving around Nashville. When he saw the billboard, he pulled off the side of the road and told his friend Gus, who was in the car, that I was going to be his wife. Gus said, "What are you talking about?" Jim said, "I'm going to marry that woman."

Gus stared at him, as if waiting for the punch line to a joke. "Do you even know who she is?" he asked. "Have you ever met her?"

Jim said, "No, but I can feel it. She's my wife." The story goes that he went home and started watching *PM Magazine* to see what kind of person I was and what kind of reporting I did. Then he cooked up the scheme of asking me to cover the event.

So I covered the story, never knowing the real reason Mr. Owens wanted me there. He called a couple of weeks after the story aired and said, "That piece was so good, I want to take you out to lunch." I accepted. Lunch turned out to be dinner and we have been together ever since. He didn't tell me until two years into our relationship about the billboard prophecy because he was afraid I would think he was odd and leave. And he still claims that he knew all along that I was going to be his wife.

I do consider it weird, but I later verified the story with his friend Gus. I prodded him, "Come on, admit it, did you two cook this thing up just to make Jim sound romantic?" Gus said, "No, I thought at the time that Jim had lost his mind and didn't know what he was getting himself into." So I believe them.

After we started dating, Jim began to talk to me about a series of shows that he wanted to do. He was interested in having me write and host them. Now, most TV people would think it risky to leave a network affiliate for an independent production company that did country music shows (at a time when country music had not yet begun to boom). Normally to move up, a television personality needs to stay with an affiliate and go on to bigger cities, eventually stepping up to the network level. But my gut instinct said "Go with him and do these shows." I loved doing *PM Magazine* at Channel 2 but with Jim, I had the opportunity to take charge of writing a pilot, then produce and host the shows.

I left *PM Magazine* without one bad feeling. I was willing to jump in and take the risks with Jim, knowing that if our ventures didn't work out, I could always get a job. Stations in Miami and St. Louis had called, so I knew I was in demand.

I was twenty-seven when I married Jim Owens. He was forty-six. It was his second marriage and my first. I had been hosting and producing one of his shows for about two years. I didn't get involved in the business end of his operation in those early days. I had enough to do. And I think because of the twenty-year difference in our ages, Jim had to make sure where my heart was.

There was the whole scenario of the younger woman marrying the older, wealthier man simply for the money, or the status. And since we had all those rumors going around about us in the beginning, I didn't really want to get into the business side, or the finances. I was more interested in helping the company grow and in doing good things for country music. We were a good three years into our marriage before I started to help make the business decisions.

I was naïve about television production in those early years. I had never written a pilot in my life. But after Jim hired me, I wrote two thirty-minute pilots for *This Week in Country Music*. Jim syndicated that show in nearly two hundred cities across the country, based on the pilots I had written. He told me what he wanted and I did it, not through any brilliance on my part, but simply by persevering. A lot of the work was awful, and when anyone said "This is horrible," I would press them to tell me what was horrible so I could make it better. I had a real craving to improve.

Jim and I make great working partners. He's very much an idea man and I am very much a detail person, which works out beautifully. He comes up with an idea and I get specific about how to pull it off. I write a treatment and bring it back for him to review; I don't remember ever thinking that what I was doing was complicated.

As the years went by, Jim put more of the responsibility on me because he knew that I would take care of the things he didn't necessarily enjoy. He likes to be creative. For example, when there was some hiring or firing that needed to be done, he would ask me to do it. My duties expanded as the company grew. In time I was a department head, then I became a co-owner. Now Jim and I run a multimillion-dollar company that employs nearly one hundred talented, creative people.

For a lot of couples, this would be far too much togetherness. But we don't fight about the things that other married people say they fight about. We don't fight about where to go for dinner. We don't fight about money or the house or cars or whether he picks up his clothes. We don't fight about his paying attention to me, or me to him. I guess the only thing we ever argue about is my impatience. Jim is laid-back; I'm a real go-getter. Both of our personalities need to be tempered, so we try to learn from one another.

Mainly, our disagreements are about work, and the timing of things that need to be done. When I see something that needs to be changed or fixed, I want it done right then. Jim wants to reflect. He wants time to play the hand and then make a decision. That approach can be hard for me to deal with, but it works for him.

His nickname in the music business is Gentleman Jim. He has been a successful television producer for over thirty years. He has a quiet way of getting the job done, without the stereotypical high-pressure antics that are so common in TV production, where temper is often confused with leadership. I am proud of the respect so many people have for him.

We often laugh and say that if we didn't work together, we could be a textbook example of a good marriage. We truly enjoy being with each other. We both love to travel, especially on our motorcycles. We enjoy eating out and going to movies. On Saturday mornings, we lie in bed and talk for hours, and on Sundays we get up and fix big pancake breakfasts. There are times when we sit side by side for hours without saying a word, each engrossed in our own book. Luckily, we have been able to share the same basic personal and professional goals.

Jim's greatest gift to me, besides his love, has been his willingness to let me grow. Unselfishly, he has helped me see how far I can take whatever talents and skills I have. Not once have I sensed any jealousy from him toward my career. He lets me be me, which sounds very simple, yet is one of the most difficult things to do in a close relationship.

I'm sure dealing with "me" is not always an easy task—for the reasons I have described. It goes against my nature to pull back on the throttle. I have always tried to keep stretching myself. This is why most of the books that are stacked beside my bed are self-improvement books. I read a lot of biographies and autobiographies in order to learn from other people. I feel that I grow when I understand the hardships other people have faced and how they handled them. It is refreshing to hear someone else's philosophy about life. I drink in all these experiences and ideas.

Norman Vincent Peale once wrote that to succeed you have to "throw your heart over the bar." He picked up that expression from circus people. When they learn to swing from one bar to the next, they may be nervous, but they know they can't just sling their bodies out there and *hope* to grab the next bar. They have to *know* they can do it. I relate to that wisdom. Whatever I do, I try to throw my heart over the bar.

I have been told by my friends that I'm very resourceful, that I am basically a self-sufficient person who can use whatever is at hand to get myself out of whatever mess I am in. Until one of them made this observation to me, I hadn't viewed myself in that way. But it rings true. Whatever tools are available, I will find and use them. I have gotten to the point where I don't worry so much about what's going to happen. I figure I can make things work out. That isn't ego talking. I believe you have to have faith in yourself because life is going to slap you across the face from time to time.

A lot of people want something handed to them, and if they get it they don't ever want to let go. Whatever level of success or fame I've had, if it all disappeared tomorrow I think I could go some place else, start lower down on the pole, and eventually climb back up. I may be fooling myself, but this is what I believe. If I believed less, I don't think I would be here today—on national television, sitting to the right of Charlie Chase.

The Last Rooster Fight

If I wasn't born to do what I am doing, I didn't miss it by much. I performed on radio for the first time at three, pulled a regular shift on the air at thirteen, and passed the test for an FCC license a year later.

Most of us would be happy to know what we want to do with our lives by the time we were thirty. I mean, that would be like lifting sixteen tons of worry off our backs. But me, I was just your typical, thirteen-year-old career disc jockey and all-purpose announcer from a small town who's now been asked to tell about his life in a book.

I've always considered myself a journalist and interviewer rather than an entertainment personality; someone who gets other people to talk about their lives. So when it came to telling my own story, I didn't know where to start. I decided to just take a step back and more or less interview myself.

Rogersville, Tennessee, is a small town sixty miles northeast of Knoxville. I was born there on October 19, 1952, at Lyons Hospital, a tiny building on a side street converted long since into apartments. Not a very impressive place, but in Rogersville if you weren't born at home that's where you were born.

When I was growing up there the population was only two thousand; there were only twenty thousand in all of Hawkins County. Rogersville was, and still is, the kind of place where a person can walk the street with no fear for his safety. Residents can stay out past dark and walk the sidewalks and enjoy front porch visits. Everyone knows everybody and it's likely that their grandparents knew your grandparents.

We were a lower-middle-class family. My dad's name was Rex. I never did call him Dad or Daddy. I called him Rex. He always liked that. My mother's name was Leafy Fatal—how's that for a fine southern name? Everybody called her Faye. Of course, to me she was just Mom. I have one brother, Ron, who is ten years my elder, and his old friends in Rogersville still call him Bones.

My mother and father worked very hard. Rex was into a lot of things but his primary business was a produce house. The townfolks called it the Chicken House because it was there the townspeople dealt poultry. My dad also had a used furniture business in one side of that same building. It was common in those days, in small towns, for a fellow to have several businesses going at once.

Mom was the first female rural mail carrier in Hawkins County. She drove her own car to deliver mail to the farmhouses on her route. After several years, she gave up the job to stay home and take care of my brother and me. Later on, she worked as a waitress at two or three of the restaurants in town. Everybody knew my mom.

We lived in a four-room house on Burem Road. There was a kitchen, a living room, a bedroom, and another small room at the back of the house where my brother and I slept. One of my "chores" was to take the rent money—$35.00 a month—over to our landlady, Mrs. Odum.

Though we never had much money, we always ate well. We had a good-sized garden and we all worked it. It was my job to go in and pull out all the weeds and an occasional snake. We had potatoes, cucumbers, and green beans from the garden, and Mom was a great cook. Plus she'd make butter-milk biscuits almost every night. Those were the best biscuits ever made. To this day, it's just not a meal without biscuits, and I always think of Mom when I eat some.

Our family attended East Rogersville Baptist Church. One Sunday, when I was perhaps three years old, as the collection plate was passed I dropped in a $100,000 play-money bill. I had kept the bill wadded in my little hand all through Sunday school, through the sermon, until the offering at the end—for about two and a half hours before I put it in the plate. My parents thought it was the cutest thing. The Lord must have appreciated the gesture because from time to time throughout my life I've been sure that the "Big Guy" was looking out for me.

The WRGS radio tower went up in 1954. It was one of the first radio stations in that area. Everyone listened; it was their new friend. Our house was adjacent to the radio station property. As a toddler, I became fascinated with the flashing red light at the top of the tower, pointing out the "radio pole" to everyone I talked to. I made a point of seeing whether I could see the pole wherever I was in town.

When I was about three I made my first appearance on WRGS. There was a blind piano player named Harold Carmichael who had a show every Sunday afternoon. Mom took me to the station to watch Harold do the show. One time when we were there, he asked me if I had anything to say or if I wanted to sing. And the next thing I knew someone had stood me on the top of the piano. Everyone was looking at me. I was the only child in the room and I was scared to death.

Tennessee Ernie Ford had a big hit at the time with "Sixteen Tons." It was the only song that I could sing all the way through. "Sixteen tons and what do you get? Another day older and deeper in debt." About halfway through the song I started to have fun and the fear went away. That was my first introduction to broadcasting.

There was no rush of Hollywood agents calling and I wasn't drafted by scouts for the Our Gang comedies, but at that moment, I was the proudest three-year-old in Hawkins County.

When I was born my feet were turned inward. I can't recall the medical term, or the explanation, but I have been told that what happened was the result of my being a big baby. Mom was a tiny woman and I guess I didn't have room to develop properly. The doctors didn't have the options they have today to correct the problem I had. About the only thing they knew to do for this kind of condition was to put a brace on a kid when he got to be about three years old.

Mine was a full-body brace, a harness that came up to my chest and was strapped all the way down my legs to the ankles. As awful as this contraption sounds, and as unpleasant as it was to wear, it worked. Today my feet are straight, although the brace pressed against my lower back and left me slightly swaybacked. As a result, I still have occasional lower back pain.

I wore that brace for about three years, around the clock. I had trouble sleeping at night, waking at all hours. Finally, the brace came off just before I started school. How I hated it at the time, but now I feel blessed that my parents had the foresight and patience to provide me with medical help. After I was in school, I got to know another little boy whose feet were worse than mine had been. His family did not seek help for him because their religion said they should not interfere with the way God made him. He grew up in pain, perhaps crippled.

I learned a valuable lesson from that experience: Sometimes it is worth going through a little suffering to make things right.

I can't say how much the brace had to do with it, but I grew up with a soft center, what some might call a gentle streak. My father's hobby was buying and training fighting roosters. I never did like or understand that sport; the whole thing was so brutal. But around town everyone talked about Rex's roosters. He trained them just as if they were athletes. He had a sort of exercise lift made from an old bed that he kept in a side room of the Chicken House. Rex would put a rooster on this thing, with his hand under the rooster's chest. The feet would hang free and my dad would make the rooster run. He did that to build up the rooster's stamina.

One of my jobs was to crush glass into fine bits and mix it with chicken feed. The crushed glass and feed mixture was then fed to the roosters. Rex said it was his secret for making the birds "meaner 'n hell." I guess it worked. There wasn't a rooster around anywhere that could beat Rex's roosters.

He took me to one rooster fight in Newport, Tennessee, which is in Cocke

County. The location of fights was supposed to be secret—because cock fighting is illegal. The way to find the fight was to follow strings that had been tied to trees. You'd follow the strings to what seemed like the back of nowhere to someone's barn. There were bleachers, refreshments, everything!

I think the local law enforcement agencies knew these fights went on. But these were just a bunch of "good ole boys" who weren't hurting anybody, so they just ignored them. I can't say for sure that this was true, but that's the impression I got.

When it was time to fight, Rex slapped spurs on his rooster. The fight was over in two or three minutes. The birds fought until one of them was dead.

It was such a bloody sight I never wanted to go again. I was glad that I'd saved the money Rex had given me to bet on the fight. At seven years old, I probably wouldn't have been able to live with it. Just having seen it was bad enough. I can't go hunting now because of that memory. I have no desire to hurt any living creature. Maybe I feel this way because of the brutality I witnessed as a kid.

It strikes me as ironic that the same man who fought roosters also loved pets, and treated them with the softness of a child stroking a calf. At one time we had twenty dogs in the house and around the yard. We even had a fox and a raccoon. Since Rex thought of himself as a patriot, when he found a wounded eagle, he nursed it back to health. He viewed it as a symbol of our great country.

Certainly we were poor by today's standards. The majority of the people around had much better homes than ours. We didn't get indoor plumbing until I was eleven—I'd go to the outhouse or up in the woods. None of that bothered me; I didn't care about a bathroom or a house. I was always comfortable.

My brother, though, got upset once while he was in high school. Not having an indoor bathroom meant if you wanted to bathe, you'd fill the kitchen sink with water and wash yourself. Ron became upset that all the other kids had those things and he didn't. He couldn't have parties at our house because there was no bathroom. A really heated argument took place between Ron and my mother over this situation. I think it was the social pressure that finally brought easygoing Bones to such an outburst.

I didn't know what a shower was until I traveled with my brother to Virginia where he had a job interview. I was nine years old the first time I ever saw a shower or stayed in a hotel room. I was very impressed to say the least, but the experience didn't make me think less of our house when I returned home. I was glad to come back to our little house where I could play with my pets and my friends.

We didn't have the toys or games to play with that kids have today. But I had the advantage of an active imagination. One of my favorite pastimes was to paint a big S on an old bath towel and pin it to the shoulders of my shirt. I'd run like a bat through the yard and then up the front steps and then dive off the porch. It was great fun. I never had any trouble entertaining myself or anyone who happened to be coming down the road. I dreamed about being Superman. Most kids did. I think today kids dream of starting their own computer software company and taking it public.

The social climate of Rogersville in the early sixties enabled me to have a great deal more freedom than kids do today. A parent could let a child walk to the store and not be concerned. I was allowed to go to ball games at the high school alone from the time I was eight years old. I could hang out with my buddies during the games and have a good ol' time. The only rule was that I had to be home before dark.

Our family had a recipe for "home brew" that had been passed down from the late 1700s by our ancestors who lived on Beach Creek. Every now and then we'd brew from fifty to one hundred gallons of this drink on the back porch and bottle it in glass soda bottles. My job during the operation was to be the bottle capper. Each bottle received a copper cap applied with an old manual capper.

Rex never sold any of his "special recipe." He kept it for company in an old refrigerator on the back porch. Of course, a lot of "company" came by to sit on the back porch with my ole man. I tasted home brew once when I was a kid and haven't touched it since. It doesn't taste as glamorous as its legend implies.

My dad was a good-hearted man, loved by everyone who knew him. His friends still tell me stories of his lending a helping hand to a lot of people and giving folks money when they needed it though he had little to spare.

For all my dad's kindness, he did have one really big problem: He drank too much. Who knows what makes someone become an alcoholic. Perhaps it was the pressure of constantly trying to eke out a living from small-paying jobs, or maybe he was bored living in such a small town. I have been told that he drank to relieve the chest pains that sometimes came to him. I will never know. Whatever the reason, he scared me when he drank. Then, as time went by, my mother kept him company. They would go on drinking binges that lasted two or three days. Then a long, quiet time would pass before there was another.

When my folks drank, they turned angry. Sometimes they would argue all night. That was when my brother, as he started driving, would fetch me and we would hop in the car and head to my grandmother's house to wait it out. I have no recollection of this scene, but my aunt once told me that when I was about six I tried to stop my parents from arguing. While I was trying to get between them I was accidentally struck in the head. I needed several stitches.

They must have felt a terrible guilt, but their attempts to stop drinking never succeeded. I remember how frightened I was the day Mom and Rex were taken to a treatment center to dry out, watching them drive off. I remember being afraid to go back into the house to get my clothes and teddy bear so I could stay with relatives.

Drunk parents make scary times for a child. During one binge, Rex broke a bottle in the kitchen and accidentally cut his right forearm just above the wrist. Blood was pouring from the cut, but Rex wouldn't let anyone near him. He sat at the kitchen table, holding a .45 automatic, threatening to kill himself or anybody who came near. The Rescue Squad—the forerunner of 911—came and finally took him to the hospital after he passed out.

He landed in jail once or twice for being drunk and disorderly, another time for firing his gun in the yard. I still have his old .45. I can't explain even to myself why I kept it; maybe for sentimental reasons. It has clear handles where he had pasted pictures of me, my brother, Mom, and Aunt Cecile.

I realized long ago that some of the things Rex did were wrong. I try not to let those parts of him bother me. I try to remember that deep down he was a big, kindhearted guy who couldn't deal with his own demons. I have tried to forgive him and just move on.

When I was ten years old, Rex died of a heart attack. The date was April 10, 1963. He was fifty-one. His death was especially hard on me because I found him. At the time, my brother was working in Virginia, so there was only Rex, Mom, and me living at home. We had a morning routine. Rex would get up, turn on the TV, and then shovel coal into our warm morning stove. That stove was our only source of heat in the house. Then Mom would hang my cold blue jeans, the ones I was going to wear that day, on a hanger near the stove. (One of the most important lessons I learned in those days was never to put on cold jeans. They froze your butt off.)

That particular morning was different. My dad had fallen asleep on the couch in the living room the night before, nothing unusual. Mom and I were sleeping in the middle room of the house. But he wasn't up and about when Mom woke me. She said that Rex hadn't answered her when she called out to him. We both knew something was wrong. Mom told me to go into the living room and check on him. I realize now that she was afraid to go herself and wanted me to be the strong one. (She became more dependent on me as the years went by.) So I walked into the living room with Mom kind of shrinking a few feet behind me. Rex was dead. He was wrapped in a quilt so his body was still warm.

It was about six in the morning and Mom became hysterical. She screamed for me to dial the four-digit telephone number for the Rescue Squad. They came quickly, but there was nothing they could do for Rex. They said he could not have been dead for more than thirty minutes when I found him.

The way people in a small town, especially our small town, rally around when someone loses a family member is really a beautiful thing to see. There's always someone there glad to help with arrangements or offering to put up out-of-town relatives. Everyone tries to give what comfort they can and everyone shows up with something to eat. It's a southern tradition.

Rogersville is situated almost in the middle of Hawkins County. Most of my dad's relatives were from an area on the county's edge known as Beech Creek, which is ten to twelve miles from downtown Rogersville. In those days most of the county roads were still quite rugged. So since many of Rex's family and friends had no way to get into town, there was one service in town and another held at Beech Creek Baptist Church. The coffin was opened at the grave site so that the folks on the creek could pay their respects.

My father's funeral was the first I'd ever attended. I don't think I understood what had happened until the coffin was shut and being lowered into the ground. Then it crashed in on me that he was gone. I was scared. I didn't know what was going to happen to Mom and me.

It is tough when you grow up without a father. I didn't have him to take me to baseball games, fishing, or camping. I had always been an independent kid, but I enjoyed spending time with Rex. I learned from him. He taught me that when you are somebody's friend, you try to be a friend in the true sense of the word. That doesn't necessarily mean you write somebody a check. It means that you try to be there when that person needs a shoulder to lean on, or someone to talk to on the phone in the middle of the night.

When I think of my dad, I concentrate on the good times. I think of Rex every day. I wish he could have known my kids. He would have spoiled them rotten. I wish he could have known there were such good things in store for me. I still miss him.

After Rex died, my brother, Ron, joined the Air Force. He was assigned to Texas, to Nevada, then California. Mom and I couldn't afford the air fare to visit him. It was four years before I saw him again. After he was discharged, he became my role model. I was always trying to please him.

Mom and I both went to work after Rex died. Mom got a job as a waitress. As conscientious as ever, she worked even when she was sick because she didn't want to miss those tips. I did whatever I could; there were not that many ways for a kid to make money. I started with a paper route, mowed lawns, and secretly gambled on the pinball machines in the back room of the restaurant where my mom worked. I didn't earn much money, but I made enough to buy my own jeans and pay for my lunch at school.

In 1964 Mom and I moved to a small but new house on Waterson Street. Mom managed to pull together a small down payment on the $9,900 home. She paid on that house for twenty years until it was all hers.

When I was twelve, Mom gave me an inexpensive set of drums. Some friends and I wanted to play music. We called ourselves the Routines and played local gigs that would make us about five to ten dollars each. Big money!

Those drums were how I got into radio. Our band didn't have a tape recorder and we wanted to hear how we sounded. Mark Beal, the manager and owner of the local radio station, ate often at the restaurant where my mom worked. Mom asked him if our group could come out to the station and record. Mark said, "Tell the boys to come on out some evening after sign-off and set up and I'll turn on the recorder."

WRGS signed off the air at sundown. We went to the station early one evening. When I walked into the studio and saw all the equipment I thought it was the most fascinating thing I'd ever seen. I asked Mark a lot of questions about how everything worked. Before I left that evening, I asked Mark whether he needed any help. He said, "I don't know. We'll see."

About three weeks later when Mark came into the restaurant, he asked Mom if I'd be interested in some part-time work, and that's how I started working at WRGS when I was thirteen years old as an "on air" intern. I loved announcing. (My voice was already quite deep.) Often I stayed long after my shift trying to learn everything about the equipment and how the station ran. I worked closely with Mark's son, Gary, and his nephew, Philip, in learning the basics of broadcasting. (Incidentally, Philip now owns the station.)

In January 1967, after three months of study, I hitched a ride to Knoxville with three others to take the test for a third-class FCC license. As it turned out, I was the only one who passed. I got my license which enabled me to operate the station solo, alleviating the necessity of a licensed operator being in the building with me. When an afternoon slot came open at the station, I got the job because I was the only licensed person available. At fourteen I had a full-time job for the grand salary of $1.10 per hour. I felt I was set for life!

Before long I was working both mornings and afternoons. I'd get up at 4:00 A.M. and ride my bike a couple of miles to the station to turn on the transmitter at 5:30 A.M. and sign on the air at 6:00 A.M. At 8:00 A.M., Mavis Livingston, the office manager who later came to be my second mother, would drive me to school.

My teachers arranged my schedule so that I had the last period of the day free. Mavis would pick me up at 2:30 and I would go back on the air at 3:00 and work until sign-off at sunset. My workday would end anywhere from 6:00 until 9:00 P.M. depending on the time of year.

On mornings when there was bad weather or snow, the local police would pick me up at home and take me to the radio station. How did I rate that personal service? Because everyone in the area relied on that radio station for information on school closings and road conditions. The station was the central focus of everything going on.

I loved those weather-emergency mornings. It was a great responsibility to coordinate all the incoming information, and it was also very exciting. I'd work with what information I had and then say, "Hey, everybody! What else is going on? Call and tell me if you have any important news to pass along." Surprisingly, everything that came in was legitimate. People wouldn't call in bogus information because they realized how essential that information might be to people's jobs and businesses.

On those mornings, I would stay on the air until Mark Beal or another announcer could get into the station. The police would then come back to pick me up and take me back home. Somehow, my work never interfered with my education or ability to keep up my grades. I was very involved with school activities and I was class president one year.

Luckily, I had some great teachers who encouraged me to keep everything going. One of my favorites was Mrs. Mae Brooks, my sophomore English teacher. She would listen to me on the radio every morning. In those days the announcer did everything from introducing records, reading commercials, and giving weather forecasts to making public-service announcements and reading the news and the obituaries. When I arrived in her class, Mrs. Brooks would have written in the corner of the blackboard any words that I had mispronounced that morning. She'd help me go over them and also mention news items that I'd read that she felt it would be helpful for me to know more about. It is difficult to imagine how different your life might be if not for the help of friends and relatives along the way and teachers like Mae Brooks who pushed and nudged you to the next plateau.

I had my first date with Karen Moles, who has been my wife for nearly twenty-four years, on July 4, 1967. We were both fourteen years old. Karen and I had ridden the same school bus all during the previous school year. I would walk past her and sit in the back of the bus and watch her until she got off at her stop. One day, near the end of the school year, I got up my nerve and sat down in the seat next to her. To my shock, she hit me with her notebook. Something clicked and I immediately decided that was the woman for me. I know it sounds like something out of *The Far Side* comic strip, but that's the way it happened.

It was several weeks before I found the additional courage to call her and ask her out. Her dad answered the phone and asked who was calling. When I told him who I was, he said that she couldn't talk and hung up. I figured that he thought I wasn't good enough to talk to his daughter.

That, though, wasn't the case. He thought I was too *old* for her. My voice was unusually deep for someone my age. Her parents had heard me on the air and thought I must be in my twenties at least, and there I was making a move on their little girl. They didn't believe Karen when she insisted that I was only fourteen. (Our birthdays are six months apart.)

When Karen realized what the problem was, she dragged me to her home one afternoon and said, "Here he is." Her dad gave Karen a look and said "I've got you figured out. You're going to tell me this short, skinny kid is Charlie and then you're goin' to sneak off with that old guy from the radio."

I stepped up and said, "Hello, Mr. Moles," in my best radio voice. At the sound of my deep voice his mouth dropped open and his eyes rolled in disbelief. And he let us start dating. He also became a great friend.

My romance with Karen lasted all through high school. We were both very strong personalities and would fight like cats and dogs one minute and make up the next. No matter what was going on, Karen was always very supportive and encouraged me more than anyone. She was sure that I could make something of myself in broadcasting. She'd go to the library for me when I needed books to research a school paper and get her dad to give me a ride to work when the weather was too cold for me to ride my bike.

I asked Karen once why she was doing all this for me. She told me that she was sure that some day I'd be famous and if I ever won some kind of award she wanted me to be able to say something nice about her. Frankly, I think she could have negotiated a much better deal.

I interviewed my first big star, Jeannie C. Riley, when I was seventeen. Her bus driver's brother lived in Rogersville and as their tour bus passed through town her driver wanted to stop and show off the bus and Jeannie C. Riley to everybody. Mark Beal called one evening and asked if I'd like to interview Jeannie. I thought he was kidding. "No, seriously," he said. "She's going to be here."

At about one o'clock in the morning Jeannie C. Riley got off the bus and I did an interview with her. "Harper Valley P.T.A." was number one at the time not only in the United States but around the world. I couldn't believe I was getting to do an interview that other radio people would kill to do. Even at that time of night Jeannie was gracious and funny. I've still got a tape of that interview and a picture that I had taken with her.

So, in a way, my career as an interviewer started with Jeannie C. Riley's bus driver's brother. Which goes to show you, the right connections can make or break you.

I graduated from Rogersville High School in June 1970, ranked 37 in a class of 157. I wasn't the valedictorian and I had always known that there wouldn't be any money for college. I knew that I'd be heading straight out into the world, so to speak. And I still felt that I had a lot going for me.

A few days after graduation I started working at WKIN Radio in Kingsport, which is about a thirty-minute drive from Rogersville. We played contemporary rock. Olivia Newton-John, Creedence Clearwater Revival, Janis Joplin, and Three Dog Night were artists who were hot at the time in this format.

During my years at WRGS I had worked long hours, most of the time without any supervision. It came as a great surprise that after I'd worked at WKIN for only a few weeks representatives from the Labor Department showed up to inform the station management that since I was underage, they were required to have an adult in the control room with me at all times, provide me with a twenty-minute break every two hours, and limit my workweek to a certain number of hours. I thought I was done for and the teasing from the rest of the DJs was endless. But station manager Lew Sadler proved willing to work with and around these requirements for the next three months until my eighteenth birthday.

Mom still needed my help so I still lived at home. I'd drive back to Rogersville after my shift and get home about 8:30 or 9:00 in the evening. I'd eat and spend some time with my mother, then go over to see Karen at her dad and mom's house. I was usually so tired that I would fall asleep on her sofa shortly after I got there. Karen would let me sleep until *The Tonight Show* was over and then wake me up and send me home.

On my eighteenth birthday, I registered for the draft. It always scared the hell out of Mom that I'd be called up. My brother was in California and had his own family. If something happened to me, she wouldn't have anyone. This was during the height of the Vietnam War. In the draft lottery my birth date was number 157 and war was escalating. I was so sure that I would be called that I constantly worried about what would happen to Mom, Karen and me, my career, everything.

But I never got called. I don't know if some kind soul at the local draft board knew how badly my mother needed me at home or if it was just plain luck. I have the deepest respect and gratitude for the guys who did go to Vietnam. I would have gone if things had come to it; I wouldn't have skipped to Canada like many young men in our country were doing at that time.

I had been working at WKIN about a year when the music director of WKGN in Knoxville passed through Kingsport on his way to a funeral and heard my show. He was going to be leaving his job at WKGN and knew that his station was looking for a replacement. He told the station management about hearing me; I was asked to send in an audition tape. As it turned out, I didn't get that particular job but the program director called me about three months later and said that they had another opening. He said, "We want you for this one."

I thought I had hit the big time when WKGN, a pop and rock station, hired me to be on the air from three in the afternoon until seven at night. Often, though, I'd stay an hour or so after my shift and then make personal appearances. So, while my working hours didn't seem that long, in reality I put in ten- to twelve-hour days.

Karen and I had been "officially" engaged for about six months. She had started attending business college in Kingsport because we planned to live there after we were married. We decided that she would finish out the semester and then transfer to Knoxville. I moved into a real dump of an apartment on Alcoa Highway and went home on weekends during the fall to visit my mother and to see Karen.

Karen and I were married on December 11, 1971, at the First Baptist Church in Rogersville. I was nineteen; she was eighteen. Our wedding was very modest, costing Karen's parents a grand total of $200, including Karen's dress. There were about seventy-five people there and we had the reception in the basement of the church. I thought it was a great wedding—but then it was the only wedding I'd ever attended.

Karen had threatened not to marry me if I didn't move out of that apartment on Alcoa Highway. We found and rented a much nicer two-bedroom house in south Knoxville. Our "much nicer" house had a stove with only one working burner and no driveway. We parked our Volkswagens in the alley in front of the house. Several mornings each week we'd have to get up early to move our cars so that the garbage truck could get through.

About seven or eight months later, my shift was changed to evenings. Karen had graduated from business college and entered the work force. She was coming home from work about the time I was going in to work. It's no joke when I say that we waved to each other in the middle of Gay Street Bridge as she was coming in and I was going out. That schedule was pretty tough on newlyweds, but somehow we made it through. We still get a charge out of looking through the notes we wrote back and forth during that time. Her notes are full of passion and sweet nothings. My replies include: "Dear Karen, we're out of mayonnaise and butter."

Eventually I was returned to the afternoon shift and promoted to music director. It was my job to decide which records were going to be played on the air and to deal with the promotion people from the various record companies who came in to push new records.

In the radio industry, WKGN in Knoxville was considered a breakout station. We were not afraid to start playing a record that had not been proven. Stations in major markets like Atlanta, Dallas, Los Angeles, and New York would keep an eye on us to see what artists and records we were playing and what kind of listener reaction we were getting. We rated that kind of attention because in New York, Los Angeles, Atlanta, and elsewhere the stakes were so high that they really couldn't afford to risk taking on an unproven record. If they played the wrong records, listeners tuned out. Lost listeners meant lost rating points and lost rating points meant lost revenue from advertisers. Rating points were important for stations like ours and WBGN in Bowling Green, but the larger-market stations had to be a little more careful with their play lists.

Record label representatives called once a week to ask what records we had added or dropped. They also kept track of how well records from their particular labels were doing so they could file their reports with their national office.

I added Bill Withers's "Lean on Me" to WKGN's play list in early 1972. Later, it went to number one and I was presented with a gold record by Sussex Records in appreciation. We were in early on some of the Led Zeppelin and Elton John music. We got a gold record for "Listen to the Music" by the Doobie Brothers and we were playing Albert Hammond's "It Never Rains in California" very early as well. I would say that about 80 percent of the time when we went with a record early we were right.

In 1974 I was promoted to program director. I handled scheduling, promotion planning, hiring of on-air personalities, and anything else having to do with programming. It was a big load and a large responsibility for a twenty-two-year-old but I was surprisingly comfortable with the situation. After all, by age twenty-two I'd already had nine years' experience.

FCC regulations were very strict at that time regarding what was said on the air. Those regulations have relaxed somewhat over the years. Fifteen or sixteen years ago if I'd said some of the things announcers say today I would have been out on my ear. The change in standards concerns me a little. Kids are able to flip to some stations and hear really explicit language. DJs talk about everything from cocaine to condoms with all sorts of sexual innuendo in between.

WKGN was one of several radio stations in the Mooney Broadcasting chain owned by George Mooney. (George had been the play-by-play man for the University of Tennessee football broadcasts prior to John Ward.) In the latter part of 1974, he received an attractive offer to buy his Knoxville station and decided it was time to sell. I was fortunate enough to be thought of as a key person in George's chain, so he transferred me to WMAK in Nashville.

I started working the afternoon shift in Nashville in November. I stayed at the Hall of Fame Motor Inn. Karen followed a few weeks later after staying in Knoxville to sell our house and organize the move. She drove to Nashville in her Volkswagen Beetle with our cat, Vittle, and our miniature dachshund, Nichols, chasing each other all over the car the entire trip. "You wouldn't believe what I've been through," she complained when she arrived. The cat scratches on her arms and the mess in her car told me that she was not very happy right then, so I didn't brag about what a great time I had had exploring the city over the past few weeks.

I've noticed over the years that it's usually the wife who stays behind when the family makes a move. She handles details of sorting, packing, and closing down the house while the husband goes on to the new city and leaves all the headaches associated with moving behind. Hey! We know what we're doing, but, of course, we hear about it later.

Over the next year and a half, I flourished at WMAK. It was exciting living in Nashville. The announcers made appearances at malls and charity events. Artists like Barry Manilow and Steve Martin dropped by the station when they were in town for concerts and chatted with us on the air. At that time, WMAK was the number one–rated station in the city. I maintained great ratings for my shift too.

Then, in 1976, the atmosphere at what had been a great working environment started to change. The station had a turnover in management. The new general manager liked to drink and took a less serious approach to running the station. The quality of the station began to suffer. Really good announcers were starting to move on.

The new manager announced to the staff that he was bringing in "a great new morning drive personality" who would also act as program director. As we later found out his great new guy was an old buddy of his who'd been out of work for six months and also loved to party. The first two weeks this personality was employed he didn't do the morning shift or any air shift— supposedly because he wanted time to familiarize himself with all the facilities. I filled in on the morning shift during this time. The morale of the station continued to drop. I started dreading getting up and going in to work.

At about eight o'clock one morning I received a call from our new morning man while I was doing my show. I could tell that even at that early hour he had been drinking. He told me that he wanted me to put his call on the air so that he could promote his new show. I asked, "Are you sure you want to go on the air?" "Hell yeah!" he said. "Put me on and we'll just do something." He babbled on, drunk as hell, for about five minutes.

When we were off the air and the next record was playing, he said he wanted to have a late breakfast with me after the end of my shift. I drove to his apartment to pick him up at about 9:30. He staggered down the sidewalk to the car. I really didn't get a lot out of our conversation during breakfast and it wasn't clear why he wanted to meet; he certainly didn't want to be my buddy. When I got back to the station to finish up before taking off for the afternoon I noticed that the general manager was acting a little strangely toward me.

I mentioned these weird happenings to Karen when I talked to her on the phone that afternoon. She said, "I think you're being set up for something. You better watch your back."

Karen wasn't saying anything to me that I hadn't already thought about. I'd realized days before that I'd let things ride long enough and that I should start looking out for myself. Thank goodness I'd always maintained good relationships with other radio industry people in Nashville, because when I finished my air shift the next day, the morning man/program director called me into his office and fired me.

Fired? The word stung. I couldn't believe it and couldn't get a concrete answer as to why. Me? Fired?

I collected my belongings and went home. I called Karen at work to give her the news. She said that she couldn't stay at work after hearing news like that and that she would be coming home.

While I was waiting for Karen to get home I sat alone in our den and thought about all my options. I wasn't really concerned about finances. We'd always been careful. We could make it for a while. Would we have to leave town in order for me to find another job? How would Karen feel about having to leave her job? I'd never been fired before. I felt lost. I couldn't believe the industry I loved was doing this to me. I'd always been told that if you worked hard and cared about the quality of the job you were doing that things like this just would not happen.

News of my firing spread like wildfire through the chain. I started hearing from all the other program directors in Mooney Broadcasting. They knew I was no slouch. They knew that something was seriously wrong for me to get fired. One even threatened to quit if this was the way the company was going to treat its personnel. I was touched by the support I received and it helped to relieve some of the anger that was building up inside me.

I also was hearing from Nashville radio people. My word, I'd only been gone from WMAK for a few hours! News of Nixon's resignation hadn't spread this fast! One of the people who called was Ted Johnson at WSM Radio. Ted had shown some interest in me earlier because Pat Sajak (now the host of *Wheel of Fortune*) was planning to leave radio to concentrate solely on television. Ted asked if I could come over to WSM to talk. I was just about to leave when Karen got home. She had me wait long enough so that she could iron my favorite shirt.

I called home a few hours later to let her know that I had a new job at WSM for an even better salary. It was probably the shortest unemployment in history.

I called George Mooney in Knoxville the next day. "George," I said, "I just wanted to let you know that I had a wonderful experience and got a very good education working in your company." When he asked me what I was talking about, I explained that I'd been fired by his general manager and program director. "I love your company," I went on. "I've worked for you for five years and been very loyal and you've been good to me. I think you need to be aware of what your management is doing. I'd monitor them if I were you." (WMAK went down the tubes shortly after that conversation.)

At the time I was fired, I thought it was one of the worst things that could ever happen. As it turned out, it was one of the best breaks of my life. I wound up with WSM, the most powerful broadcasting outlet in the city. I didn't know it at the time, but my move to WSM would open the door to television, and eventually lead me to The Nashville Network.

Better Television Through Chemistry

People often tell us we have it. And there's no bigger compliment. The "it" is the on-camera chemistry between the two of us . . . that indefinable something that people say is fun to watch. Whatever it is, we're glad that so many people seem to notice.

We try to avoid comparisons, even though the TV writers always want to label us as a country music version of Regis and Kathie Lee, or Mary Hart and John Tesh. It's flattering because we respect both of those TV duos. But the truth is, we were a team before either of them. We decided a long time ago not to try to analyze our on-camera relationship. If we did, we were afraid that might ruin it. We only know that as a pair we clicked, right from the beginning. The matchmaker who brought us together was the award-winning television producer Jim Owens (who was dating Lorianne and would shortly become her husband).

Since the idea was his, it seems only fair to let Jim have the first say.

JIM: I had been producing specials, mostly, with stars like the Statler Brothers, Jerry Reed, Johnny Cash, and Conway Twitty. In the early eighties, I decided that a show out of Nashville with a concept similar to *Entertainment Tonight* would work. The country music industry was growing, and so was the interest in the lives of the artists. We played around with it for a year or so, using different formats, trying to come up with something we thought would sell in syndication.

I knew Lorianne would be right for this show because of her personality, and her ability to write and produce. The tough part was finding a partner, someone she could bounce off of, someone who would complement her. I had been watching Charlie Chase on Channel 4, WSM, the NBC affiliate here. Charlie really grows on you. He's this type of person: The more you watch him, the better you feel you know him.

I felt they would make a good combination, but the only way to find out was to get them together. They knew each other's work; she did a magazine show on Channel 2, Charlie had one on Channel 4. But they had never met. So I picked up the phone and called Charlie to see if he was interested. We set up a meeting at the Opryland Hotel to have a drink and talk for an hour or two. This was in January 1983. I wanted to do a pilot and I needed to present it in March in Las Vegas—that's where the NATPE (National Association of Television Programming Executives) convention was being held. So I had to get the pilot done by late February.

The three of us sat down and started to chat and I just watched them. They hit it off right away. Basically, they became instant friends. Had a lot of the same interests. You never know until you try something for a while how it will work, but you have to go with your gut instinct. Mine told me that they would be good together.

The show was called *This Week in Country Music.* We did a 30-minute pilot, news-oriented, with stories on Ronnie Milsap and Barbara Mandrell. We took the pilot to the convention and the stations jumped all over it. *This Week* went on the air in September 1983, and we cleared over 180 markets in a matter of months.

The original show was a newscast, with a little joking and bantering. They reported whatever was going on, births and deaths, cradle to grave. And they did it in a way that made people feel they knew them. The show has gone through a lot of different concepts and formats from where it is today. In 1986, it evolved into *Crook and Chase,* an hour, live, from our own facility (on McGavock Street in downtown Nashville). It was still a news show, but an odd thing happened. Fans started asking if they could come and watch the show. They wanted to *see* Lorianne and Charlie do the news. So we started letting in audiences, and at the same time, we would bring on one live guest Lorianne and Charlie could interview.

Some of the people at The Nashville Network couldn't understand why we would have an audience for a news show. I tried to explain that it was due to the personalities of the two anchors. Lorianne and Charlie are so good at interviewing; they put people so much at ease. That is their forte.

From the first *Crook and Chase* show, they have done what we call a "cold opening." They stand in front of the camera and chat a little back and forth. Then we hit the theme and you see them move over to the set and sit down. Each opening was unscripted and they still do it that way. No team of comedy writers. Their monologues are pretty much just the two of them. They might talk about the idea before they go on, but it's never scripted.

Jim still has his offices and studio on McGavock Street, where *Crook and Chase* went from a weekly show to a daily one in 1986. There was always a long line of fans waiting for seats winding around the corner. Jim says he knew we had our own identity the night Dottie West was to be the guest but became ill and couldn't make it. A production assistant went outside to inform the crowd, and a man shouted, "We don't mind. We're happy to see Crook and Chase." Not one person left the line because Dottie West had to cancel.

It still was unclear what imaginary line we had crossed. We considered ourselves reporters who took pride in asking the tough questions as well as the sympathetic ones. But it was hard to picture, say, Dan Rather and Connie Chung performing in front of a live audience.

CHARLIE: I didn't know either of them before Jim called. Then I started asking around: "Who is Jim Owens?" I was told that he had produced some independent television shows, some big specials for syndication. That's all I knew when we had our first meeting. I had no idea what syndication was. I knew the basis of it, but as far as the number of stations you needed to survive, I didn't have a clue.

Everything came together for the original show. Lorianne and I met three times before we went on the air. First, to talk about the idea. Then to do the pilot. The third time was when we taped our first syndicated show for *This Week in Country Music.* Now, that's fast.

LORIANNE: I think Charlie and I becoming partners was fate. I've always preferred to co-host than to host alone, and I've had good relationships. But Charlie and I got along especially well. I hear about some co-hosts clocking each other's time on the air to see if one is getting more "face time." I think it becomes obvious when co-hosts dislike each other. I couldn't work in that kind of situation. If Charlie and I didn't genuinely like one another, I would have moved on long ago.

CHARLIE: The key is, I can make her laugh. When we first started, Lorianne hadn't been in television long. I'd say something and she would start giggling. The interplay relieved some of the tension. So we have fun together. I also knew we were pointed toward the same goal. Now, we might be getting there in different ways. She moves straight ahead. I tend to be all over the road. I stop for milk shakes. But I knew we would get to our destination at about the same time.

LORIANNE: Another reason we get along well is that neither of us has an attitude. Away from work, we live totally separate lives. I think it's good that we have kept that separation. Our jobs are so intense, if we got together during our leisure time we'd spend the whole time talking about the show. That would only create problems for our families. One of the questions we get asked the most is "Do you and Charlie get along as well off camera as you do on camera?" My answer is, if a hidden camera followed us around for a week, you would see exactly what you see during the show. We joke, we kid around, we make each other laugh.

But we can also get serious. I can talk as freely and as personally to Charlie as I talk to my husband.

CHARLIE: Many of the viewers think Lorianne and I are married. When I'm asked if we are, my typical response is "We get along too well to be married." Our relationship developed over time and we understand each other. We know when to leave each other alone. We know when the other one needs to talk. We know when one of us needs some kidding. Best of all, we are able to share silence.

LORIANNE: We receive a lot of wonderful mail about our relationship. Our viewers are in on all the inside jokes that Charlie and I pull on each other. We have the best time teasing back and forth and they love to get in on it. Fun things happen with our audience during commercial breaks. One incident started when someone jokingly told me I needed to stop picking on Charlie. I said in mock defensiveness, "*Me* stop picking on *Charlie*? He's the one who tells everybody how bad my cooking is!" The audience started clapping and cheering in my support.

CHARLIE: Of course my answer to that was "Ladies and Gentlemen, I do it as a public service. Lorianne's cooking is so bad, her dog goes next door to beg."

LORIANNE: When I reminded him I don't have a dog, he said, "I know. He died after attempting to eat one of Lorianne's biscuits." But Charlie wouldn't let it go at that. He announced to the audience that I have my own cookbook coming out, and that every page is numbered 911. Then the audience was cheering for him. We all have fun with the insults. I must say, though, that Charlie has drummed up nationwide sympathy for my cooking skills. I receive wonderful recipes from people who feel sorry for me. A few have even offered to give me lessons in their own kitchens!

CHARLIE: People want to know if either of us really gets mad. That has never happened. We both know it's all in fun and we try to convey that lightheartedness to our audience.

LORIANNE: We do get close to the line, though! My favorite dig at Charlie is about his hair. Most men experience a little thinning, so when someone asks if Charlie wears a toupee, I'll say, "Absolutely not. Who would actually *buy* a toupee that looks that bad?" The audience loves it when I one-up Mr. Chase.

CHARLIE: Of course, I will not be outdone. I shuffle through the cards on which audience members write questions and find one about how nice Lorianne looks. I'll say something like "Oh, by the way, Mrs. So and So is here from Toronto and wants to know what kind of makeup Lorianne wears. Ma'am, it's Sherwin Williams Interior Latex. How many coats does it take, Lorianne?" But some nights she is the "zing queen." Recently Garth Brooks appeared on our show to announce that he was going to bury the master of his CD *The Hits* under his star on the Hollywood Walk of Fame. Lorianne quipped, "You know, Charlie, the only difference between Garth's CD and the one you recorded is that your CD was buried *before* it was released."

LORIANNE: When I get a really good one in like that I'll sometimes high-five the entire front row. With the way we go at it, it's no wonder that our relationship is the number one topic people ask us about. Running a very close second is our appearance. People seem to want to hear details about our hair, makeup, and wardrobe. I'm frequently asked if I've ever been a model or a beauty pageant contestant. That is very flattering, but I think I'm more like your average girl next door. Charlie teases me a lot on the show about my hair and makeup, but I can tell you that I *do not* spend all day primping for the show. In fact, I honestly look much like a hag most days because I'm running from one meeting to another, taking calls, and typing memos all at the same time . . . in other words I'm in my executive producer mode and my main concern is getting the show produced properly or helping to make the right decisions that our company is faced with every day. I'm sure by the time I get in the makeup room our makeup artist, Brenda Gower, and our hair stylist, Roger Estes, are thinking "This girl needs help!"

I spend about fifteen minutes in the makeup chair. I have very oily skin, so I can't wear a lot of gloppy cosmetics. Mostly I put powder over my bare skin and slap on some lipstick. Then Brenda does the real artwork with eye makeup and blush. Brenda has a wild sense of humor that turns makeup time into a comedy act. One time as Charlie was settling into the chair, he put on his best Barney Fife cocky attitude and said, "Hey, Bren, how does it feel to put makeup on a big star such as myself?" Without missing a beat she deadpanned, "Yeah, well, if you ever reach that status, I'll let you know."

It gets weird on the hair side of the makeup room, too. One day, years ago Roger and I were talking about people we know who say certain words strangely . . . like "sirk" instead of "silk," or "har-spray" rather than "hair spray." Since then we've created a whole language using mispronounced words. Some nights Roger might say something like "I'll wup yer har so it'll be fuffy," meaning he's going to brush my hair in a way that makes it soft and fluffy. I know it must sound stupid to other people but it cracks us up.

CHARLIE: Roger is anything but silly when he's at work on a head of hair. He's known as the best in town at both cutting and styling. Many of the stars ask him to do their hair for album covers, videos, and award shows.

LORIANNE: He *has* to be good to deal with my hair! You've heard of the frizzies? Well, I must have invented them. It takes Roger about forty minutes to smooth it out and put a soft curl in it. We're very open about everything he does to my hair (like highlights to cover those gray strands that are popping up!), but Roger has sworn himself to secrecy on one issue. He won't even tell *me* who he uses more hair spray on, me or Charlie.

CHARLIE: When it comes to show clothes, Lorianne and I are running neck in neck. There isn't a day that goes by without letters, phone calls, or audience comments about our wardrobe. Between shows, Lorianne and I always confer about what we'll wear next. Coordination is needed when you're viewed together on TV. Bachrach Clothing Company outfits me for each show and it's easy to choose from the extensive wardrobe they've provided. As a result of my line of work over the last two decades, my closet is overloaded with over 150 suits and nearly 400 ties that I can still wear.

LORIANNE: I'm afraid my clothing story is about as ridiculous as Charlie's. I've been in television fourteen years and most shows provided clothing that I got to keep, so I've collected a lot. These days I prefer to buy my own. My mom and I love to shop together. She's the one who picks out most of my clothes and jewelry. We shop all over Tennessee and in New York, Los Angeles, and Atlanta.

Jim and I have moved twice because my clothes were exploding out of the closets. I had wardrobe stuffed in guest room closets, hallway closets, bathroom closets, even the kitchen. I was keeping hats in the kitchen on the cup hangers! (I just know Charlie could make a cooking joke out of that.) Then one day my husband decided he needed to build a four-car garage to house our cars and favorite vehicles, our motorcycles. My eyes lit up and I said, "Why not build a second story on the garage that I can use as a closet?" So he did. We call it our "four-car closet" and it's packed to the gills. I probably have close to two hundred pairs of shoes alone, but women tell me all the time that they have a hundred or a hundred and fifty pairs. What is it with we women and shoes? My husband would like to know. I do wear everything over and over again, so it's all put to good use. I'm glad so many people say they get a kick out of tuning in to see what we're wearing each night.

CHARLIE: It's funny because we don't think about it nearly as much as they do. Once we are on the set, our priority is to do a good job and end up with a good show. We are not concerned with having every hair in place or checking ourselves out on the monitors. Sometimes Brenda, our makeup artist, gets frustrated because she misses touching us up when we are goofing around with the audience or a guest star. Hopefully our audience can sense that we care about making a decent appearance for them, but our main focus is the stars and the music.

There is no finishing school that we know of for television co-hosts. What we bring to the camera is the sum of everything we are—how we grew up, the jobs we've held, the understanding people we married. In the end, what you bring to the job is simply yourself. You can't fake it, not ninety minutes a night, five nights a week, fifty-two weeks a year.

CHARLIE: What makes it all so comfortable is that, even though we are known as a team, we each allow the other the space and freedom to be an individual. I've earned a reputation for all my antics and the stunts I pull on my *Funny Business* specials. Lorianne, too, is respected for her in-depth interviews that often deal with sensitive subjects.

LORIANNE: I see myself as a connection between somebody who has something interesting to say and those who can benefit from hearing it. My highs are when I interview someone very different from myself yet manage to form a trust that leads to an open and honest conversation. As a fan, I want to hear how others overcome life's crises, or how they find humor in everyday living. If, as an interviewer, I can help present a celebrity in an honest way to the public, I feel I'm doing my job. I feel I'm a conduit.

That doesn't mean I have to share their life experiences. I don't have much in common, for instance, with Hank Williams, Jr. But when I interview him, I feel very connected. In the early 1980s, I did what Hank describes as the first in-depth interview he had ever done, although it didn't start out that way. We sat by the lake, fishing, at his home in Paris, Tennessee, and the interview was supposed to be some small talk about his hobbies.

Hank later told me that he had braced himself for the typical reporter questions about drugs, whiskey, and women. Luckily, I was more interested in the man behind the image and my questions got past his reputation and into the real reasons he thinks, feels, and acts the way he does. He delved into his childhood and what his father's death meant to him, and what his mother's control over him did to him. Hank had the chance to explain some of his pain.

I don't always agree with what he does, but I like him. When Hank Jr. told me he thought our interview had been good for him and good for his fans to hear, it was, and still is, a tremendous compliment.

Of everything I do, I most want to be recognized for my interviews, probably because I put so much heart into them. And I'm thankful so many people seem to enjoy the banter between Charlie and me. It's funny though. I've worked from the beginning of my career to be more than just a coiffed, tailored fashion plate. I have been a videographer and a videotape editor (although my talent in these areas isn't anything I can brag about). I still write, research, produce. Yet, I often hear from people who say they tune in to see what I'm wearing. And men have written me "If I turn on the show and you have on slacks instead of a short skirt, I turn it off."

This used to bother me because I considered it a sign I wasn't being taken seriously. But I have gotten so much good feedback over the years about the interviews, the writing, and producing that I find it easier to accept compliments about my clothes or appearance. I've learned that anytime anyone thinks something nice about you, whatever it is, you should be grateful. And I am.

If I were to change anything about the way I live, I wouldn't be so one-tracked. I haven't allowed myself to have much free time. Even though my work is fun, it is all-consuming. For the first four or five years of our marriage, Jim and I didn't take a vacation. I regret that. We should have flown off to some exotic location at least one week every year. But we were building a company. It was like a fireball inside us. We just had to get it done. We didn't even realize until two or three years ago that all we did was work. That fact hit me hard one day when Jim and I were standing in our dining room, looking at this beautiful table that seats twelve people. We realized that we didn't have enough time to have dinner parties. We didn't have time to go places with people.

I think that kind of devotion is one of the reasons why we're successful, but I don't know if it's healthy for the long term. I was diagnosed in the last year with a condition that required surgery. I had a benign uterine fibroid tumor that had grown to the size of a grapefruit. It was causing me unbearable pain and bleeding. I was weak and anemic, and surgery was the only answer. But I was trying to decide when I could have the operation so it wouldn't interfere with my work schedule. I was looking at my calendar, thinking "Now, I can't do the surgery on the thirtieth because Billy Ray Cyrus is going to be on the show and he has an important announcement so I need to be here for him. And I can't have it on the sixth because Sawyer Brown is booked and they're such good friends and great guests, I can't miss them."

I was trying to determine when I could fit dealing with my health into my schedule. Our general manager Jerry Fox sat staring at me and finally blurted out, "I want to slap you. I'm having to hold myself back from slapping you." He said, "Forget the show! Burn your calendar. Think of yourself. Go get this taken care of. Why do you care which show you miss?" He was absolutely right. I don't know what it is that drives me. I have been wrestling with that issue for a long time. I had the surgery and everything turned out fine, but the incident brought up the whole issue of what should be important in life.

Jim Owens says that Lorianne is a perfectionist in an imperfect world. That has caused her some problems in the past, but she has really come out of it in the last year or two. It used to gnaw at her when she felt a show could have been much better than it was. But there are going to be good shows, bad shows, and shows that are in between. She is still learning to accept that. Charlie accepted it from day one. He understands this is not a perfect world.

CHARLIE: I want to be honest about this. We all had high hopes when Lorianne and I first teamed up, but Jim Owens assured me I could keep my day job. So I did. WSM Radio was, and still is, one of the most powerful signals in the nation. As the home of the Grand Ole Opry, and because of its reach—sometimes it can be heard as far away as Cuba and Canada—WSM is one of the real powerhouses in the radio world.

At the time I joined the staff, the station played adult contemporary music during the day and country at night, a mix that may seem surprising. The format is all country now, but back then we played artists such as John Denver and the Four Seasons. The transition to all-country didn't happen until 1978, when WSM was finally able to attract an audience big enough to sustain the ratings.

By then I had learned that all radio stations live and die by the ratings. They determine how much a station can charge for the commercials it runs, and that money pays the overhead, including salaries. It's a vicious cycle. Management will add or drop on-air personalities with every swing of the ratings. On the other side, a lot of disc jockeys move from station to station like a band of gypsies. Some change jobs the minute they're offered an extra $50 a week.

But the environment at WSM wasn't like that. I saw a maturity in the operation there that I had never before seen. There was a real commitment both from the management and the talent, which was an advantage for someone like me. If I had a question, I knew I could go to one of the veterans for an answer. In other places, if I had to ask anybody anything I felt I would lose respect.

But even at a station as secure as WSM, a person still feels pressure. Fortunately, I was able to start shutting it out while I drove home at night. Usually, I liked to have the radio on, but if I was really stressed out I would turn it off and just drive. Twice a week I played on the company team in a softball league. That was a great outlet and a chance to get to know my working buddies in a different light because we didn't talk shop at all. On other nights, I'd kick back, watch TV, read, just anything to take my mind off the job. I knew the pressure was always going to be there the next morning. I would start to worry about the ratings even as I shaved. I knew I had to get away from it because I had a wife and a personal life I needed to protect.

I worried even though I did well in the ratings. I think people listened to me because I liked to have fun on the air. My afternoon show was done with a viewpoint: "You've had a rough day so let's get silly." I knew who my listeners were. It was drive time and my listeners were business people on their way home. At that time, we had the only airborne traffic report and that gave us a special edge. I knew people tuned in for that reason and I tried to get them hooked between traffic reports. I read every publication I could get my hands on, and I would drop little tidbits of information, or talk about subjects that might be important or funny or weird.

For example, I'd give the latest stock market summary and make fun of my broker. You know, "It must have been a bad day, his secretary said he can't take my call because the telephone cord won't reach the window ledge."

I do remember a day that was historically bad, October 19, 1987, when the market fell five hundred points. I remember the date because it was my birthday. I went on the air the next day and started off by saying, "After yesterday's stock market crash, nobody could afford to pay for the birthday present they had given me, so they came and got them."

Much of what I did on the air had to be improvised. The show was live and anything can happen during a three- or four-hour shift. In the event of something major, I had to be able to react spontaneously. No contest, the single most memorable shift I had at WSM was the day Elvis Presley died.

It happened in the middle of my shift, at 4:22 in the afternoon. I was listening to NBC's internal feed when I heard the announcement that Elvis was dead. I thought "Oh my God, what do I do now?"

I switched to the network announcer for the bulletin, then reached back and grabbed the first Presley album I could find. I saw a cut that I loved, "Now or Never," and I slapped it on the turntable. As soon as the network feed was over, I came back on and said something like "The music industry is shocked over this announcement. WSM now remembers Elvis Presley," and I popped the song on the air.

I will never forget what happened next. A lady called up and raised hell because she felt the song was inappropriate. I didn't know what to say to her, but I felt just putrid. Later, Gordon Stoker of the Jordanaires told me that it was Elvis's favorite song. That lifted my spirits considerably. Maybe I had accidentally done something right, after all. I just couldn't figure out what the caller's objection was. What did she think I should have played "You Ain't Nothing but a Hound Dog"? I thought "Now or Never" seemed to be the right selection, not fast, not slow, just a soft, solid, sentimental song. We played Elvis music all night long. A lot of people who worked with Elvis lived in Nashville, and they kept calling in to offer their insights.

Country music started showing new life in 1978. Kenny Rogers and

Dolly Parton were becoming household names. Country music was a hotter topic in Nashville, so much so that WSM-TV offered me a spot twice a week doing a report on the top-selling singles and albums. "You play the records," I was told. "You read all the trade magazines. You're up to date on what's happening in the industry."

That was the beginning of my television career. I did the reports for the next four years. Every week I reported the top five–selling singles in country and pop music. I told what sections of the country were buying what records, which artists were doing well, and what the concert tickets were costing. We used one of the first music videos to be released, Sheena Easton's *Morning Train (Nine to Five)*. My reports were fairly popular. This first venture into television got me to thinking about the direction of my career. For years people had told me, "You'd be great in TV." I'd always had television work in the back of my mind. However, I'd always put these compliments aside in trying to keep to my philosophy: Don't let your ego make you look too far ahead. Focus fully on what you're doing now so that you don't mess up and that bright future you've imagined never comes.

I decided it was a good time to start taking a few more steps in that direction. At that time WSM Radio and WSM TV operated out of the same building. Work between radio and television seemed to come quite naturally; one complementing the other and helping to make my performances in each stronger. Eventually I did a few reports from University of Tennessee football games in Knoxville and sometimes worked as substitute sports anchor on the evening news broadcast. Over time I realized that I liked television and decided that I wanted to do more.

I loved working at WSM during these years. There always seemed to be something new happening everyday. New challenges popped up constantly. The only thing I didn't like was trying to work out time off around key rating periods. These occurred during the fall and winter months, so I had to take my vacations during the summer. Karen at this time was working at Opryland Park whose peak time of course is March to October, so her vacations could only be taken in the winter. We hardly had any time off together except for an occasional weekend trip.

I also ended up working the morning shift almost every Thanksgiving and Christmas. This was because I didn't have kids and everybody else on staff did. I guess most people don't really stop to think that TV and radio stations don't sign off on holidays. It's just always there. Somebody's got to work.

And when the microphone goes on, the show has to be your main focus. People don't care if you're missing your turkey. It's not their problem if you don't feel like doing a show. You still have to be upbeat. The audience is still listening, waiting to be informed and entertained.

"The show must go on" tradition hit me hard in 1980. Karen suffered a miscarriage late Christmas Eve. On Christmas morning, I did my shift while my wife, just out of the hospital, stayed home alone. We were two of the loneliest and most heartbroken people on the face of the earth.

Less than a year later our first child, Rachael, was born on November 11, 1981, just three weeks short of our tenth wedding anniversary. I had been with Karen during delivery, although I hadn't really planned to be. Whenever we had talked about the birth, I hadn't given Karen a definite answer about being in the delivery room. I secretly harbored the fear that I would faint and make a fool of myself. I figured I could make it in the labor room, but I would just hang back when they moved her into delivery.

Suddenly, things began to happen quickly. As Karen was being wheeled out of the labor room, somebody tossed me a set of surgical greens and a mask and pushed me toward the door. They sat me on a stool and told me to hold her hand. I wonder if I looked as sick as I felt. Minutes later, Rachael was born.

It was the single most remarkable experience of my life. This seemingly simple event that has been happening over and over for thousands of years affected me in a way that I hadn't expected. When I first held this beautiful child, I felt truly blessed. I cried for an hour.

Meanwhile, on the career front, WSM-TV was sold to Gillette Broadcasting in 1981 (the call letters were changed to WSMV.) The radio operations moved to Opryland Park. I shuttled back and forth between the radio station, doing my regular shift, and the television studio, working on a sort of free-lance basis. I continued the weekly music reports and sportscasting, when I was needed. I was still anchored in radio, even as I continued testing the unsure waters of television.

I had another opportunity in 1982, when I was twenty-nine. Teddy Bart, who had hosted Channel 4's midday news and entertainment show for years, decided to quit. I expressed an interest in auditioning for the host position, but instead the station hired the veteran soap opera actor, Ben Johnson.

Ben did the show for three months, then they came back to me. I finally got a chance to do an audition, and Stella Parton appeared on the show as my guest. For years after, I would remind Stella that the interview was so good that I got the job because of her.

On August 31, 1984, while I was having lunch with friends, I received word that my mother had died of a heart attack. I learned from my aunt Cecile that Mom had passed away very suddenly, but quietly, while watching television in her favorite chair in the little house on Waterson Street.

I was glad that she lived long enough to see me have a little success. I knew she enjoyed hearing people talk about seeing me on TV. When anyone loses a parent, we always wonder if we had done everything we could have for them. I hoped I had been a good son and I know she was proud of my brother and me.

After the funeral, I went back to Mom's house and walked through it alone. I'm not sure why. Perhaps I was hoping to find some sense of her there. And I think I did, a little. It occurred to me as I passed from room to room just how hard she had to work for her house and everything in it, how hard she had worked for everything in her life. I felt proud of her.

Just a little over three weeks after Mom's death, on September 25, our son, David, was born. The doctor had decided to induce labor. We laughingly referred to my hectic schedule, and Dave's birth was actually planned around a taping of *This Week in Country Music*.

This time I knew I could handle the delivery room. After her somewhat troubled pregnancy, both Karen and I were more than a little nervous. I held my breath when he didn't cry right away, but soon he began to howl—a perfect baby boy. I carried Dave to the nursery, overcome with the same emotion I had felt at the birth of our daughter. A little while later, Karen and I phoned Rachael from the recovery room to tell her that she had a little brother.

I was the host of the *Channel Four Magazine* show until 1989. I felt very comfortable with being on television. Of more importance, I felt challenged. I think it is essential to stay fresh and on top of your game in this business. I've often thought about how radio was such a great training ground for television. That experience gave me a sort of built-in sense of timing. I love talking with people, but it was all those hours on radio that taught me how to put a guest at ease. When guests are relaxed, they are more willing to reveal themselves. I was always working to make my guests feel relaxed.

On at least one occasion, I may have overdone it. Once, the late Wolfman Jack, who had dropped by to promote a big concert, was so laid-back he forgot we were on the air. We started talking about personal things, and I said casually, "You're a big-time star now. How many houses do you have? You move around all over the place. I know you have one in Hollywood. What else do you have?"

He said, "I've got a big farm in Colorado."

Impressed, I repeated it: "A big farm in Colorado?"

He said, "Yeah, no shit."

I didn't want to bring attention to what he had just said, so I said, "Okay," sort of giggled, and moved on to my next question. At the next break, Wolfman asked, "Did I say what I think I said?"

I said, "Yeah, you said, 'No shit.' "

His eyes got wide. "Really?" he said. "That's the first time I've ever done anything like that on the air." He went to the back of the studio and was nauseous, he felt so badly about it. Wolfman had been in radio forever and couldn't believe what he had said. After the show was over, I called the front desk and asked how many calls we had gotten?

The operator said we had gotten only one call.

During the first three years that I hosted the midday show, I was still on the radio. I thought it was great. I told myself "Man, this is the best of both worlds." I even got the opportunity to host the *Waking Crew* radio show on WSM during all these other assignments. The *Crew* was the second longest running radio show on the air, second only to the *Grand Ole Opry*. I was very proud of getting the host slot on a show that I had subbed on occasionally over the years. My day had become even longer; however, I had the security of radio, while I found out if I would fall flat on my face in television. If I had, I would have simply stayed in radio. But that's not what happened. About 1985, I decided TV was the way I wanted to go. I had given myself the time to make sure.

I quit radio that year because I wanted to streamline my hours. My daughter was born in 1981 and my son in 1984. They had a lot to do with my quitting radio. I wanted to be at home more.

At that stage of my life, I was real content. I felt my career had moved along. When *Crook and Chase* became a hit, I thought "This has been a pretty fast ride. But I'm on board and I'm gonna have fun with it." We had moved so fast that I had never been tempted to try to get ahead of the train. I found that if you work hard enough, the opportunities just present themselves. As it turned out, I was getting ready for another switch in the tracks.

By 1992, Nashville was buzzing with the rumor that the venerable Ralph Emery would soon retire. A new show, and a new signature for The Nashville Network, was about to open up.

Following Ralph

In Nashville, Ralph Emery owned the country music interview franchise for forty years. In short, he is a legend, just as surely as Johnny Cash and Kitty Wells are legends.

Ralph had a radio version of what TNN, The Nashville Network, is today, and he had an opportunity to befriend the stars in a way that no one else will ever have again. He had an audience that listened in every night on the clear channel WSM in forty-eight states. Dolly Parton, Willie Nelson, and others will tell you that they might not be where they are today if it weren't for Ralph Emery.

He made the same kind of impact for more than a decade with his television show on TNN called *Nashville Now*. It was *the* place for the country music stars to be seen and heard.

When Ralph announced that by October 1993 he would be stepping down as host of *Nashville Now,* some people were surprised and others weren't.

Those that weren't understood the breakneck pace he had been keeping for years: hosting several television shows including an early-morning program on a local Nashville station, *Nashville Now* of course, and various other TNN specials. He also produced and hosted his own syndicated radio show, and was writing his autobiography. Ralph once told us that he tried on many occasions to accept golf invitations from the stars, but he was so dead-tired out there on the greens he couldn't enjoy it.

Once people got used to the idea that Ralph was really leaving *Nashville Now*, rumors and rumblings began flying as to who was going to take his place. Who could possibly follow Ralph Emery? The truth is, no one could really take Ralph's place. TNN decided they must create a whole new show, with a new host.

LORIANNE: At the time, our show *Crook and Chase* had filled the first hour of prime time on the network and was the lead-in for Ralph. But when it was announced that Ralph was retiring, we heard that the network had done research on the Smothers Brothers, Pat Boone, and Roger Miller as possible hosts. Charlie and I were mentioned in this mix because our show was already popular on TNN.

CHARLIE: I guess it was logical for us to be considered by the network, but we had some real concerns. Our *Crook and Chase* show had strong ratings and had won many awards. *TV Guide* had named us "The Nashville Network's Dream Team" and *Cable Guide* magazine had voted us Entertainment/News Program of the Year. We felt we had a really good thing going. We also knew, as we do now, that it's incredibly tough to produce a successful show these days because television viewership is so fragmented. There is huge competition to get people to watch. We're talking hundreds of channels and thousands of shows! So our dilemma was very real. Do we stick with the successful and respected *Crook and Chase* show? Or do we take the opportunity for growth and challenge with *Music City Tonight*?

Jim, who was already producing a major portion of the prime-time programming for TNN, received a call from David Hall, the network's general manager, and Paul Corbin, the program director. "They said they wanted to come over and see me," he said. "They just came right out and asked if I would be interested in taking over that time period, with Lorianne and Charlie as the hosts."

What leaked out later were the results of the survey the network had taken, which were much more extensive than we had realized. First, they had polled the stars, their managers, their publicists, and the record label executives and asked "If TNN does a new show, who should host it?" We were told the universal response was Crook and Chase. Now they had to find how the viewers felt. The figures that came back were in the ninetieth percentile of every category, the highest figures in the research firm's history.

LORIANNE: When we heard that both the fans and the country music industry were behind us, there wasn't any long discussion about it. We were honored to be considered and honored to be chosen. They told Jim to create a format that was broader than *Nashville Now*. The *Crook and Chase* show had blazed new trails on TNN, and they asked us to continue that trend.

CHARLIE: This was in July and they wanted the new show on the air in October. Jim said the start date was October 18, what did we think? And in unison, the two of us went, "WHAAAT?" It was twelve weeks away! Not nearly enough time to create and launch a brand-new show. We would have to move from our downtown studio out to Opryland, where they had always produced *Nashville Now*, to a temporary structure that was ten years old—and still temporary. It meant expanding our show from an hour to ninety minutes and we had twelve weeks to get it on the air.

LORIANNE: And, of course, Jim said no problem. We could have killed him! Mainly because we had to continue doing the *Crook and Chase* show while planning *Music City Tonight*. Doing double duty on two major shows was a tremendous task. If I have a choice, I'll never attempt that again. You can only give part of your attention to two projects that each need your full attention. I cannot even begin to explain the amount of frustration we all felt in this situation.

It was like building a city, brick by brick. We had to create and build a new set, put together a top-notch band, hire a staff, refine the format for the show, and get some of our staff moved from the offices downtown to the TNN complex several miles outside of Nashville. I swear to you, on the Sunday night before the premier, I was on my hands and knees spraying mirrors with Windex in the trailer we were using as a "green room" for the guest artists. I had picked out and bought all the furniture. At the last minute, I was doing housework.

The new set had a cozy, living room setting, a "guest door" for an occasional surprise entrance, and a video wall for live satellite feeds from other locations—nightclubs, concerts, parties. Our ninety minutes would encompass the entire music scene of Nashville, not just pure country. The basis would be country, but we would not ignore gospel or contemporary rock.

LORIANNE: Just taking over *Nashville Now* was not an option. Ralph had been at the helm of that show for a decade and nobody could waltz in and take his place. As expected, we met resistance from a group of fans who wouldn't accept that Ralph was gone. Charlie and I were braced for that reaction. We knew Ralph would be missed regardless of what we did. We knew we could never take his place. And there were some viewers who let us know how they felt. We received letters pleading "Bring Ralph back." One viewer wrote that our replacing Ralph Emery was like Mount Rushmore being replaced with Mickey and Minnie Mouse. Ouch! Thankfully, those types of letters were few. To this day Charlie and I are astonished by the outpouring of support from the fans and the stars.

CHARLIE: Ralph was great about the whole transition. Toward the end of his reign, he invited us on his show after he told his fans he was leaving, and said that he couldn't think of anybody better to take over his time slot than Crook and Chase. We feel that Ralph is our friend. We've invited him to be on *Music City Tonight* several times since our show went on the air, and he's always been a fun and interesting guest.

LORIANNE: As he was a host! During one of my guest appearances on

Nashville Now Ralph asked me, and not in a critical way, if I had any *long* dresses. I said, "Well, not very many because I don't like all that fabric around me." I either wear slacks or short dresses. It's not that I feel I have great legs; actually, I'm bowlegged and I have scars all over my legs from being a tomboy. Luckily, the hosiery covers that up. And for those who have written and asked, no, my legs are not insured. But I'm very flattered that some of you think they should be.

When we took over the prime-time slot, we wanted to show that people from all different kinds of lifestyles can, and do, enjoy today's country music. During our tenure on *Crook and Chase*, many of the stars thanked us for presenting country music with class and style. I think the change we have brought to our show is a measure of what has happened with the artists. The newer artists like Garth Brooks and Reba McEntire have added lights, high-tech production, and special effects to their stage shows. They've taken steps that will appeal to a broader audience.

We have done much the same thing. A few people have said they think our show is too "slick and uptown" for country. In a way, that seems like an insult to the whole country music industry. It's as if some critics would keep all the stars in boots and jeans on a barnyard set. Garth and Reba are two major examples of how country can grow and change . . . yet still speak simply and powerfully to the heart. What that tells me is the more you stand at the forefront of change, the more you are likely to be criticized.

CHARLIE: We don't want to sound defensive. But I disagree with those who say we should "bring the music back home" rather than export it to the rest of the world. We're proud of Nashville. We're proud of the music. We're proud to display it. The image is evolving. Maybe some people are worried that the soul of country music will be lost. But that won't happen.

LORIANNE: At the heart of country lies the enormous body of work contributed by all who came before . . . Jimmie Rodgers, Hank Williams, Lefty Frizzell, Marty Robbins, Ernest Tubb, Patsy Cline, and on and on. *That* is the soul of country music—and it's much too powerful to be lost or damaged by anything that may be going on around it.

On October 18 *Music City Tonight* made its debut. There was very little time to rehearse with the band. The sound mixes needed more tweaking. Virtually up to air time, the crew was checking the lights, the sets, the camera angles. That Monday we went live to sixty-three million households, with one thousand two hundred audience members in our studio.

We're proud of what we did that night, proud of what it takes to do this show. It takes ten and a half years of experience to pull it off, and that's what we have, that's what pulls the wagon.

LORIANNE: Neither of us is the type of person who looks too far ahead. We know that what we do is important to a lot of people because they tell us so. We get tons of mail. We have hundreds of people in the studio each night and we listen to what they say. If they tell us "we didn't like this comedian, he's too off-color," we take that opinion seriously.

We know you can't please everyone. As hosts and interviewers, we want to be smooth and competent. But the viewers, God bless them, understand those occasions when our emotions get the best of us. When John Berry was a guest on our show following his brain surgery, he got very emotional talking about the letters of love and support from his fans. I could barely hold back the tears and it was obvious. My nose started running profusely, and after the segment was over I told John, "I think this is the first time I've snotted all over myself on national television." Wiping away his tears, John smiled and said, "Gee, I'm so proud to have been a part of that!" We all laughed and it was a wonderful release following such an intensely emotional interview.

The Marriage-Go-Round

Let's face it, in show business, breaking up isn't all that hard to do. Couples who work out their problems don't get nearly enough credit for staying together. Sandy and Garth Brooks, Vince and Janis Gill, come quickly to mind. The repairs are more difficult because they have to go through the wringer while the public watches.

This is an ongoing conflict in country music (as it is wherever people work in a fishbowl). Among the stars in general, there's a certain amount of getting drunk and sleeping around that may seem acceptable, even colorful. Yet they play to an audience, especially among an older generation, that believes mightily in the Ten Commandments. The fans can deal with this inconsistency right up to the moment they discover that someone is getting hurt.

What Garth and Sandy told us, in private and on the air, took courage. He admitted he was unfaithful and had to beg her to take him back. As Charlie put it, Garth had to grow up and return to the real world. When you have the kind of success he has experienced, even the most mild-mannered fellow tends to see himself as bullet-proof.

Humility is a hard lesson to learn, but we all learn it one way or another. Sandy and Garth made it through the tough times. It probably helped that their relationship started in an unconventional way. Garth was working as a bouncer at a bar in Stillwater, near the campus of Oklahoma State University, while both were in college. Sandy got into a fight in the ladies' room and he was called in to break it up.

LORIANNE: When I did one of my first interviews with Garth and Sandy together, he was reluctant at first to talk about this encounter. He said, "My wife is a lady. I don't want people to think of her any other way." But Sandy didn't mind. She said some other coeds had been hassling her. She got tired of it, threw a punch and ended up putting her fist through the bathroom wall. (That may be a commentary on her strength, or on the thickness of the bathroom walls in the average nightclub!)

Both were giggling by the time Sandy finished the story. Garth had to enter the ladies' room to bounce Sandy out of there, and she made an impression on him. She had been a lifeguard that summer, she said, so she had a deep tan and her hair had been bleached almost white by the sun. Her tan and her hair were especially noticeable that night because she was wearing a black outfit. Garth said he took one look and went "Whoa!" He told her he was the bouncer and said, "Well, honey, if we throw you out, we gotta make sure you get home okay!" Smooth move, Garth! As he put it, he not only deposited her at the dorm, "I tried to walk her up to her room, and I tried to walk her *into* her room! I don't believe in love at first sight, but I just couldn't believe how cute she was."

Even in college, he admitted, Garth had a reputation as a womanizer . . . something Sandy was well aware of, which is why she declined his offer to escort her to her room. In fact, she told him right to his face, "I've heard about you, Garth Brooks." But he kept chasing her and finally she did go out with him. They fell in love and got married. Sandy really believed Garth could become the star he wanted to be. She followed him

LEFT: *1958. My first birthday. See! It was all Mom's fault that I fell in love with prissy clothes.*
FAMILY COLLECTION

BELOW: *1962. My sister, Kim* (left), *me, and my brother, Bret. Mom's "little angels."*
FAMILY COLLECTION

ABOVE: *1963. My sister, Kim* (left), *and I lived at dance school. I wasn't that good, but I loved to dance.*
FAMILY COLLECTION

LEFT: *1975. My senior year photo. On picture day, we all prayed for no zits!*
FAMILY COLLECTION

LEFT: *The 1978 Miss Nashville Pageant. The good news: I made it into the top ten finalists. The bad news: There were only twelve contestants!*
FAMILY COLLECTION

BELOW: *January 26, 1985. Jim and I were married in the Presidential Ballroom at the Opryland Hotel.*
FAMILY COLLECTION

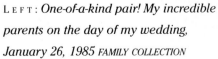

LEFT: *One-of-a-kind pair! My incredible parents on the day of my wedding, January 26, 1985* FAMILY COLLECTION

ABOVE: *Our dear uncle Floyd. His illness and recent death from brain cancer is an unmendable heartbreak.*
FAMILY COLLECTION

RIGHT: *1984. A favorite photo. My husband, Jim, and Conway Twitty had just won an award for their TV special, "Conway on the Mississippi."*
OWENS COLLECTION

LEFT: *A young Charles Chase, age three months*
FAMILY COLLECTION

BELOW: *Charlie at age five in Rogersville, with my dad, Rex, and pet goose, Oscar*
FAMILY COLLECTION

ABOVE: *In 1956, age four, Charlie shows us the proper way to hold a dog. Notice our "outdoor plumbing" in the background.* FAMILY COLLECTION

RIGHT: *Fall 1963. After the loss of my father, I looked to my brother, Ron, as my role model.* FAMILY COLLECTION

LEFT: *Mom and me about the time I started working at the radio station in 1966.* FAMILY COLLECTION

BELOW: *May 1971. Karen and my engagement photo* FAMILY COLLECTION

BELOW: *Bill Withers presents me with a gold record for "Lean on Me."* (Left to right) *Wade Conklin of Buddah records, Charlie, Bill Withers, and WKGN program director, Bob Baron* FAMILY COLLECTION

back and forth from Oklahoma to Nashville as he tried to put together different bands. As his plans, one after the other, fell apart, Sandy tells us her belief never faltered.

One dramatic day Garth literally lost control. Sandy said he was crying, banging his head with his fists, and she was terrified he was going to hurt himself. She started screaming and crying too, hitting him in order to make him stop hitting himself. And she managed to blurt out the words that would give him strength and hope. Sandy told us, "I said, 'Garth, you have the talent. You have all the talent in you. But it's not just going to come to you (meaning stardom). You've got to go get it. (Her voice got more forceful.) You've got to go out there and *get it*.' " Outside of his immediate family, there's nobody who believed in Garth more than Sandy.

CHARLIE: These are two of the nicest people anyone can ever meet. They are not self-centered. They are very caring. They seem to have a fine sensitivity to one another. I think that's why the marriage has survived. His affairs happened. It happens to people in all walks of life.

I think it happens more in the country music field because the fans are so hands-on (no double meaning intended). Most artists believe that being accessible is an important feature of the business. There's a close bond between the fans and the entertainers. It can become very difficult for them to know where to draw the line.

LORIANNE: I think when they first married, Garth needed someone to lean on, someone to say "Yeah, you can do it and I'll help you do it." But he also admitted he worried that marriage would tie him down. Then he became a star and unfortunately he broke his vows. The stories got back to Sandy. She heard about him looking out in the audience, pointing, and saying, "I want her, and then I want her."

I'm not defending that kind of behavior, but I've traveled with stars on their buses and seen them backstage. I am amazed how groupies just throw themselves at the artists. Some of these girls are beautiful and voluptuous. Now, you would like to think a performer is strong enough not to partake of this "babe buffet" as we call it. But I can understand the temptation.

When Sandy found out, she called Garth on the road and confronted him on the phone. She said something to the effect, "You better get home if you want to save this marriage because my bags are packed." As they tell the story, he was onstage that night singing his hit song "If Tomorrow Never Comes." It was just Garth and his guitar, and as he sat singing on the edge of the stage, the words of his own song began to haunt him . . . "if tomorrow never comes, would she know how much I love her . . ." He says he began to cry right there, and out of the crowd came a voice, from someone who could not have known about the phone call from Sandy earlier. The voice rang out "Go on home to her, Garth!" Right then and there, Garth said he got up, walked off stage, and headed home to Sandy. She did, indeed, have her bags packed and she laid it on the line. She refused to look askance at his adultery. Garth said he cried, and literally got down on his knees to beg her to stay. That was the turning point in their relationship.

CHARLIE: A confrontation like that can be a rude awakening. Those wounds may never completely heal, but they know their relationship has been tested and it seems stronger because of it.

Of course, Lorianne and I don't do marriage counseling. We don't compete with the tabloids. We don't do trash TV. We have an obligation not as critics, but as reporters, to treat them as fully dimensional people. We wrestle with the questions we ask, and when to ask them.

LORIANNE: I asked Sandy, "Why did Garth make the choice to stay in the marriage? Why did he choose to come back with you rather than continue to his 'point and come hither' routine for the rest of his life?" Bless her heart. Her lips started quivering and she said, "The only way I deal with it is he keeps coming back to me. I've got something they don't have. I know what's inside him. Because I don't love 'Garth Brooks.' I love the man. He has a heart of gold, and in my heart I feel if I would ask him, he would do anything for me."

I think Garth felt ashamed of his past behavior because he kept looking at the floor while Sandy spoke.

CHARLIE: There are some other success stories in this business. Vince Gill and his wife, Janis, have endured. When you see those two in public now, you can tell their emotional bond is probably stronger than ever. I think that may have been the result of their both having known success. Not only has Vince been successful, but Janis has the satisfaction of being part of the Sweethearts of the Rodeo. The one with the tough road in that situation is their daughter, Jenny. She has to be a strong kid with two parents in the same career, but in different acts, each going and traveling in different directions. The fact that Vince, Janis, and Jenny are able to hold all of that together says a lot about each of them.

LORIANNE: Vince and Janis have been through some of the most trying times a couple can go through. They married young and both were struggling for recognition. Vince hit first with the group, Pure Prairie League. When that group dissolved, he came to Nashville to be a session player and a harmony vocalist for other stars. In fact, I remember I was doing a television piece on Tanya Tucker, in the recording studio. She was cutting the vocals for a song that became a big hit for her, "Just Another Love." Vince showed up to sing harmony. He was incredible and Tanya told him he was going to be a big star someday. Others were saying the same thing . . . that it was just a matter of time. But it turned out to be a long time.

Vince landed the record deals and released the singles, but for years he didn't get the hits. Meanwhile, Janis struck it big in the late 1980s with Sweethearts of the Rodeo. Her career moved right past his. Vince has been very honest in admitting that, at times, it was tough to watch her success. It hurt, he told me, because "everything I had done prior was completely washed out the window. I'd had a top five record with 'Cinderella,' a couple of top tens, the 1984 Best New Male Vocalist award, a lot of great things. And her career jumped right up. Everything I'd done seemed to just get pushed completely aside. But the only envy I ever felt was probably for the lack of my own success." He said he resented her being away from home and not being there for Jenny. When they both talked to me, Janis was in tears. But she made an important point. Vince is *not* the kind of guy who thinks the "little woman" should stay home to clean and cook. He was always behind his wife's career, but he was deeply concerned about Jenny not having a normal home life with both parents to raise her. He felt real frustration. Then the tables turned. Sweethearts of the Rodeo faded a bit and there came Vince, zooming past her on the music charts.

CHARLIE: Literally, they passed like ships in the night. It's tough to try and maintain a healthy marriage or a romance. Take Vince. Female fans adore him. Some envision themselves in the arms of Vince Gill. They think of him singing to them, they imaging the dining and dancing and fulfilling of their fantasies. At times, the relationship between the entertainer and the public is bizarre. He doesn't want to destroy the illusion, but as an individual he knows he can't live up to these visions. The public feels that it owns a part of Vince Gill. But for him to maintain any kind of a personal life, he has to let them know there are boundaries.

LORIANNE: Vince has made it clear that his marriage is sacred, but the realities of the country music business have made some dents. All of a sudden, Vince was the rising star, the one who was gone from home all the time. Janis found herself stepping back and feeling her own resentment. She admitted, "I felt like I was given a lot of grief, a real hard time by Vince when you look at the way things are now. Vince is gone twice as much as I ever was. Being a woman in the business, there's a lot of double standard. I'm not talking about Vince in particular, but across the board. It got pretty tough at one point. I remember wondering if we were going to be able to pull this thing off."

CHARLIE: When we see Vince on an award show, thanking his daughter, Jenny, for her inspiration, and he gets tears in his eyes, he's sincere about that. He's onstage and looking down at her and it's probably the first time he has seen her in two months. She is in her early teens. These are the formative years that parents hate to miss. Being away from each other and their daughter has to be the biggest strain in the world for both of them. But the key is, I think they have dealt with it to the best of their personal abilities.

LORIANNE: In interviews, when they start talking about how they feel about each other, they choke up. I've had to wait so they could compose themselves. Yet it's really sweet to watch them work because he treats her so gently. Vince is known around the industry for being so good his peers call him a "quadruple threat." He's a great picker, singer, and song-writer and a good-looking man. Janis has admitted to me that musically she's intimidated by him. Whenever she writes a song, she is shy about letting him hear it. She said she so desperately wants him to think that her work is good. It would break her heart if Vince criticized her as a singer or songwriter. Because she's sensitive, they worked out a deal. If Janis wants his advice, she asks for it. Only then does he tell her his opinion of her work. Vince says he tries not to criticize, rather, he gives suggestions for improvement. Well, I wanted to know from Janis if Vince was as ideal as he seems. I said, "Okay, all of these female fans think Vince Gill is the perfect man and that you must be the luckiest woman on the planet. I want to know the truth about your home life." The only clue she would give me, which I thought was kind of cute, was how sloppy he is. She said, "I have to follow him around the house with Dustbusters, one in each hand, cleaning up after him. He leaves dirty clothes, under-wear, and socks everyplace." She added that Vince eats all over the house and leaves a trail of crumbs and dishes everywhere. She joked, "No wonder he likes me to stay home. It would be a pigsty if I didn't!"

CHARLIE: There is a teasing side, a lot of good-natured ribbing when one is on our show without the other. And you can see their fun side backstage, just jabbing one another. I think that takes a lot of pressure off the marriage and their careers. But I'm not sure I would want to be married to a singer or songwriter. Look what happened when Vince and Janis went through some troubled times. They had a serious argument and he went to see his friend John Jarvis. They ended up writing a song about what had happened, "I Still Believe in You," and it became a number one hit for Vince. But then everybody knew about their argument.

Having the kind of show we do is a little like running a house of mirrors. You see the stars onstage, in their armor, and you see them offstage with their guard down. Sometimes you try to protect them and the fact is they don't always want to be protected. Meanwhile, you want to be fair to the viewers but not pander to them.

LORIANNE: Other couples in the spotlight have made their relationships work, too. Every time Waylon Jennings and Jessi Colter are together, to me they look like newlyweds. He has her hand in his, or he is playing with her fingers. He will look at her and pull her hair back away from her face so he can see her eyes. The look on his face is like he's melting inside. They have been married more than twenty years and they still treat each other like that.

Let's not forget that Waylon is the original outlaw. He told me he loves women and says, "I appreciate everything about them." Jessi is a strong lady and doesn't tolerate any nonsense, which is probably one of the reasons they are still married. She told me that during the first ten years of their marriage, neither one of them had a clue about what was going on. Their love was the foundation, but they spent years working through their differences, reaching an understanding.

When Waylon was in his outlaw period, it was generally known that he was into drugs. Just a couple of months ago, Waylon was co-hosting *Music City Tonight* with me, in Charlie's absence. About an hour before the show, Waylon and I were both in the makeup room getting "pouffed and powdered," as Charlie calls it. I was getting my hair done, and Waylon was in the makeup chair next to me. Somehow our conversation had turned to his old drug days, and off the top of his head he started throwing out dollar figures as to how much money he used to spend on cocaine every day. Mind you, he wasn't bragging. He was talking matter-of-factly about a part of his life. My show rundown for that evening was on my lap, so I scribbled down the figures Waylon had mentioned and calculated it. It added up to more than two million dollars! Can you imagine? Two million dollars, right up his nose. When I told Waylon, even *he* was surprised.

Willie Nelson recently said jokingly that Waylon hasn't been much fun since he quit his wild ways. Waylon himself admitted to me that he was "one funny son of a bitch" when he was high. And it is true, the stories they tell from those days are just hilarious. I could listen to them all night long. But personally, I'm glad that, these days, our outlaw is healthy and happy, and that he and Jessi are going strong. And by the way, it's my opinion that Waylon is one fun guy to be around, even without the drugs. Especially without the drugs.

CHARLIE: Jessi stayed with him through all of this and somehow something brought them together. There was no tragedy, nothing like that. Maybe it was because their son, Shooter, came along. Regardless of what happened, they are a fun couple to observe now. He has such respect for her. She's a strong woman who expresses what she feels and Waylon listens.

It's amazing what people tell us. There probably isn't another business in the world where people reveal so much of themselves through their work. Actors don't. They are always playing someone else. You can have the same person handle your taxes or insurance for years and not know much more than his phone number. But most musicians will just rip out their hearts and hand it to you. Take country legend George Jones. The pain he's lived through can be heard in every note he sings. He had not been successful in marriage. So who would have guessed that marriage would save not only his career . . . but his life.

CHARLIE: When George and his wife Nancy first got married, some were saying, "Ho hum, here goes another George Jones marriage. How long is this one going to last?" But these two are apparently a match made in heaven. They have been together over a decade now. On the show, we gave them a wedding cake on their tenth anniversary. We wanted to do that because when George and Nancy married they didn't do anything special. They were down at Jones Country, the park he had in Texas. As I heard it, after the ceremony they stopped at a Burger King and then went back to the ranch.

LORIANNE: Nancy told me that they were broke. George says no more than $20 between the two of them. They had enough cash for a burger, but they had to split it. Yet in those early years, a lot of people questioned her motives.

CHARLIE: That relationship saved his life. Nancy turned George around. It's not that she is awed by him. But without this lady, I don't know where George Jones would be today.

LORIANNE: Nancy didn't know George was a famous country music singer when they met. She had heard of him, but didn't know much about him. George was playing at some club, and as a favor to a friend who was dating one of his managers, Nancy went to this performance. Nancy saw that he was drunk most of the time, but she realized it was partly because there were some bad people around him who were in control of him. She started feeling for him. She decided she was going to try to help him.

Nancy told me, "I saw the inside of George. The outside was somebody else. The inside of George Jones is a great person. Warm and loving. But the man wasn't being treated right, he was wanting out of what he was captured in." George has said he believes some of his so-called friends and managers were stealing from him, but he didn't have the strength to break the ties. He admitted to me that he didn't appreciate Nancy at the time, but he knows now what she did for him.

It took a long while, but she eventually ran off all those people and the other women. At that point, George told her to leave him alone. He couldn't see that Nancy was his real friend, not those other people. To get him off the alcohol, she fixed a mixture of Tylenol and water and made him drink it. I don't know where she got that idea, but this was how she weaned George from liquor.

I remember the first time I met her. She and George were at our studio and he was doing some sort of a television public service announcement. Nancy was on a phone outside my office, raising her voice to somebody on the other end: "George Jones is a legend and you are *not* going to treat him like this. You may have done this in the past, but I'm not going to allow it anymore." I don't know about the person at the other end, but she certainly got my attention. I thought, "Yikes, she is like a lioness guarding her cub." I never would have guessed that she and I would be friends as we are today. I have a tremendous amount of respect for her and I thank God she has the courage to stick up for George that way.

CHARLIE: At that point, Lorianne and I were thinking, "Here is a lady who has taken over the job of not only managing George's career but his life. Can she handle it?" Little did we know then what she had done to save this man. We just didn't know all the story at that point. She is another of those strong-willed women, who seems to know what is best for George because she knows him so well. This is an example of a trust between an artist and a manager that is rare . . . unless the two people are married. But what did George have to lose? He was already nearing the brink of self-destruction. He went into the hospital suffering severe withdrawal. He told us he was sick for two years, but Nancy stuck by him until he kicked his addiction. It was a blessing in disguise when those two got together.

LORIANNE: Nancy was a waitress and a divorced mother when they met. I thought to myself, "Now, wait a minute. Nancy has come in and seen something in George Jones that nobody else has seen, at least, not lately. She has fallen in love with him and decided he was worth saving. But, in order to save him, she had to take over not only his personal life but his career." So I asked her, "How does a waitress figure out how to write up multimillion-dollar contracts? How did you deal with promoters and record label executives?" And she said, "Everything that I have learned about the business I learned from George Jones." George chimed in, "It worried me at first. She's got one of them Cajun tempers, and you don't want to get people in Nashville mad at you." Nancy countered, "I was so protective of George, but my temper is better now. I've learned a lot."

I've often wondered about women who fall in love with troubled men. My husband says that women are attracted to the outlaw type because these men seem dangerous and exciting. Maybe this is true. I think some women have the ability to see beyond all the bad things into the real soul of a man. They see the good in him and they break down all that macho, beer-drinking, hey-babe kind of thing. Jessi Colter and Nancy Jones are that kind of woman.

CHARLIE: Whatever the reason for the attraction, it certainly worked out for George and Nancy. I've never seen them together when either one was depressed. They are always up, bright, and cheerful. Of course, she still has to keep an eye on him. He will still do things like buy or trade cars without her knowing it. I heard he was trading cars once a week there for a while. He has several now. All the plates have "No Show" on them. There is "No Show 1," "No Show 2," "No Show 3," and on up to "No Show 7." He has a DeLorean that a fan gave him. He calls it his "Bat Car" because the doors open up to the top. Occasionally, he can be seen driving around in that car in the role of superhero, fighting crime and defending the community. The right car is important in the hero business. Do you think being George Jones's wife is a full-time job?

LORIANNE: He has a genuine love and respect for her. I remember once when I needed an interview with George, Nancy told me to call her at home on Sunday. When I did, she called him to the phone, "Honey, Lorianne wants to talk to you." I heard George in the background say, "Aw, Nancy, I'm watching the football game. Tell her to call back." Nancy said, "Now, George, she's called to talk to you." George is grumbling in a tongue-in-cheek way, "Aw, Nancy," but he treks to the phone and says, "Darlin', I'm watching the game, so let's hurry up." Nancy had returned to the kitchen where she was cooking up a big pot of beans and some cornbread (one of George's favorite meals), and I could hear her in the background calling out suggestions for the scheduling of our interview. It's touching the way she looks out for him.

I think one of the reasons they bought a farm was to give George a place to go and tool around on his tractor. George told me that for some reason, he just enjoys mowing the grass. Charlie and I are trying to get him to come mow our yards! He loves that farm. They lived in this subdivision down the street from Charlie and me. George had let Nancy decorate the house and it was beautiful—done with pastel colors. But he just got antsy living there. So she said, "Honey, why don't you buy a farm?" And he did.

CHARLIE: They both seem to get satisfaction from that place. When he's in town, George goes out there bright and early every morning about six or six-thirty, checking on his cows.

One of the reasons many think George and Nancy have endured is because they are both focused on his solo career. That wasn't the situation in his earlier relationship with Tammy Wynette. A lot of stress had to be caused by them trying to manage two careers in one marriage. They started battling professionally, and those battles damaged the personal side.

LORIANNE: Tammy Wynette has talked to me about this. She said that when she met George, she was looking for stability. She was emotionally insecure at that time, and had already been through a couple of marriages. Plus, she was a single mom trying to get a career going. But George was admittedly unstable too. He was having substance abuse problems. They were two needy people. When you put two dependent people together, who can't answer each other's needs, things can get messy. From what they've each told me over the years, George Jones and Tammy suffered really deep wounds. They obviously didn't understand each other's needs. But all of that is behind them now. Each found someone to fill whatever need was there. George has Nancy. Tammy has George Richey, who brought her the stability she was always seeking.

People have asked how Nancy and Tammy get along these days. I once asked Nancy that question. Her exact words were "I don't have a problem with Tammy." But Nancy said that she doesn't necessarily agree with everything Tammy says. For example, she said it hurts when Tammy talks about George's past behavior because George has changed and shouldn't be judged by his past. Nancy says that she tries to overlook those comments because of the family ties and the children. She and Tammy are cordial when they see each other.

CHARLIE: An even tougher role may be the husband who is willing to be married to a famous woman. In a lot of cases, men do not usually have a secure enough ego to deal well with a famous wife. With that in mind, I have often wondered how Ken Dudney adjusted to being the husband of Barbara Mandrell. Ken always worked with Barbara and the band. It had to be tough having strangers call you "Mr. Mandrell."

LORIANNE: I asked Ken that question. He told me that it didn't bother him the slightest for people to call him "Mr. Mandrell" and that it happened all the time. His attitude was that if somebody addressed him that way, it just shows they care about Barbara. He takes it as a compliment.

Her fame is not a problem for him. Barbara has always given Ken a tremendous amount of credit for helping to manage her personal life and her finances. She can depend on him emotionally because he is very practical and logical. Barbara once told me that earlier in her career (I assume as she was approaching superstardom) her schedule was becoming more than she could handle. She frantically told Ken, "I have eighteen major things to do today. I can't get it all done!" She said Ken looked at her and said calmly and deliberately, "One thing at a time." Barbara blurted out, "But I'll never get it all done, I've made commitments and I won't be able to come through . . ." Without flinching, Ken repeated, "One thing at a time." His advice to her was to stop thinking about everything she had to do. Start with the first task, give it your full attention, finish it, and move on to the next. Barbara says it's that kind of commonsense guidance from Ken that keeps her focused when she has a schedule that's unbearable. It's obvious that it works for them when you consider all they've accomplished over the years.

CHARLIE: Maybe one of the secrets to a successful marriage in the entertainment business is for the spouse to be involved with the artist's career. Ken and Barbara have been fortunate because he can be with her and in most cases they were able to bring their kids on tour when they were young. It is rare for an artist to have a successful career while keeping the family together, so that he or she can retire and look back upon it with pleasant memories. Bless them if they can pull it off. I don't know how they do it.

LORIANNE: You start with someone who is very unselfish. Ken Dudney is always thinking about what is best for Barbara. The times I have been in her home, typically Barbara was running around and trying to find Ken on the intercom. The sound would be blaring all over the house: "Ken, Ken, where are you?" He'd come trudging in and say, "Barbara, you don't have to scream to find me. You've got the biggest voice of any woman I know." He laughs at moments like that, and it's obvious how deeply he cares for her.

Their marriage works, he says, because he knows what Barbara loves to do. She needs to be on that stage. And he doesn't resent it. He does anything he can to help her get in front of her audience as often as she can. Likewise, she does loving things for him. She buys him special gifts like the new Huey helicopter she surprised him with one year. Not long ago he wanted to go back to college to get a master's degree in business at Belmont University. She supported him all the way. One day when I was at her house for lunch, Barbara proudly showed me some of Ken's homework and textbooks. It looked quite complicated. As famous as she is, she went to his graduation and sat in the audience with everybody else to watch her husband get his degree. It was *his* turn to walk across the stage and accept the applause. Afterward, she threw a huge party at their home in his honor.

One of the sweetest love stories in country music is Jimmy Dean and Donna Meade. We saw it all unfold. I was doing a special with Jimmy Dean, so I flew to Rhode Island where he keeps his yacht. Besides all the hard work, Jimmy really showed us all a good time. We cruised the waterways, sipping champagne and eating fresh shrimp. Jimmy kept us all entertained with stories about his experiences in show business. At one point, Jimmy looked at me and said, "Hey, I saw a girl named Donna Meade on *Nashville Now.* What do you know about her?" I had been around her a few times and said she was nice. He made a few more comments about her being pretty and having a beautiful voice. And that was the end of it.

A few months later, Charlie and I happened to be guest-hosting *Nashville Now,* and Donna Meade was on the show. By this time my special on Jimmy Dean had aired and Donna had seen it. She called me into her dressing room and said, "I just wanted to tell you how much I enjoyed your show on Jimmy Dean. He's a very special man." She went on to tell me that she had received a fan letter from him. She told me some of what was in the letter. He complimented her on her talent and had encouraged her in her career. I could tell she was incredulous that a star of Jimmy's stature had taken the time to write her. It dawned on me that something big was happening here.

It turns out that Jimmy called Donna and asked to meet her. Their relationship grew from there. He had seen Donna on television and fallen in love. I think it must have been love at first sight. (Kinda sounds like the old Jim Owens billboard story, doesn't it?) My husband and I have known Jimmy for a long time, and I will tell you that he has been a different man since he married Donna. Before, he was still a fun guy, but I sensed some sadness or loneliness underneath. Today he seems like such a happy man. Jim and I went to their wedding, which took place in the garden of their home. They both cried so much during their vows that everyone attending started giggling because it was so touching. Donna calls him her "cowboy." He calls their relationship "the sweetest thing I've ever known." They have been married for several years now, yet when they are on our show and she is onstage performing he watches her on the monitors with a lovesick look on his face. He'll lean over to Charlie and me at least a couple of times and say, "Isn't she the prettiest thing you've ever seen?" They are precious to watch. So perfect together. It was wonderful to witness their love story as it unfolded.

The common factor for all the couples we've talked about is that nobody keeps score in these marriages. There is a huge amount of give and take when it comes to relationships that work. When it's there, it is a lovely thing to see.

CHAPTER 7

Road Kill and Bus Toys

It would be hard to overstate the importance of the bus as a symbol, as well as a form of transportation, for country bands through the years.

Today many of the stars travel in motor homes that are custom-made and equipped with sleeping quarters, showers, satellite TVs, microwave ovens, and fax machines. Whereas the buses of yore were beasts of burden, like camels, the modern buses are more like yachts of the highway.

In the early days of Roy Acuff, Merle Haggard, and Johnny Cash, the bus served as the nerve center. The boys in the band sometimes slept in their seats at night and hung their laundry from the windows. For many musicians who grew up in the south, anything with an engine drew their interest—from hot rods to pickup trucks. Some claimed they could tell by the vibrations of the road what town they were approaching. At least one member of every band was a fairly decent mechanic who could come within fifty miles of guessing when the motor would need an overhaul.

The bus is part of the history and the myths of the business because it was, and still is, a symbol of the open road. It was then, and is to a slightly lesser extent today, a life for gypsies. They work hard, play hard, and frequently manage to find the humor in the tedium around them.

CHARLIE: When I go backstage at a concert, I'm often surprised at how many people have been cleared who don't seem to have a reason for being there. Eventually, I'll find out that the artists or their managers have given them access just to hang around. Let's face it. When these artists are out on the road making a living, they are away from their spouses. They have desires. They get lonely and there isn't much to do. They find themselves onstage, looking down in the audience and seeing attractive women of all ages. The women are starry-eyed. If given an opportunity to go backstage, they more than likely will jump at the invitation. It's a chance beyond their wildest dreams for them to be personal with the stars even if it's by offering themselves. So the temptation is there. The opportunities are there. It's just whether or not the artists succumb and take advantage of it. Since stars appear on our show, we had to deal with this regarding our own backstage admission to *Music City Tonight.* Now we have a pretty tight control on the backstage area, but it used to be that there were people who had no business being there, except for the social aspect . . . if you want to call it that.

LORIANNE: I'm not going to name names, but we have heard that there are certain singers who have either a manager or a roadie or someone in the band whose job it is to scan the audience and choose the proper ladies to meet the band backstage. Perhaps nothing happens. Maybe it does. But these designated spotters are on the lookout to get companionship for the artists.

I was talking to a band member recently and he told me that he was getting ready to marry his ex-wife for the second time. I said, "What's different now? What will make it work this time?" He said, "I finally decided to stop playing with bus toys." I was about to ask him what that meant and it hit me that it was another term for "groupies." I've also heard them called "slut puppies." Whatever you call them, his unfaithfulness had broken up his marriage. I've talked to several of the stars about this. Johnny Rodriguez told me once that it was very difficult to be on the road, with multitudes of women offering themselves to you. It's hard to say no.

CHARLIE: Let me point out that we're not saying that every young lady who goes to a concert is going there for that purpose. But included in the mix who attend are those who are hoping to enjoy more than the music. It's not that every time they go backstage it leads to romance. I don't know. I do know there are more than a few willing participants on the road. I've gone to my share of concerts and it doesn't take a rocket scientist to figure out what is going on.

LORIANNE: I've asked myself why a young woman would want to have a one-night stand with an artist. I daresay that most of them realize that's all it will be, a one-nighter. I guess it gives them some sort of self-worth to be able to tell their girl friends they slept with or hung out with a country star. I think it's because Americans are celebrity crazy. *Entertainment Tonight, People* magazine, *Music City Tonight,* we all celebrate stardom. We help create stars.

CHARLIE: It is a situation aching to happen. When these artists are away for so long, they become more vulnerable. Their guard is dropped. But in another way, these liaisons still surprise me. What is to keep these women from going out and bragging about all this, and the information getting back to the artist's record label or his management—not to mention his wife, if he has one. Keep in mind, this is a business. Touring is not supposed to a social activity. There are so many risks involved for the artist, not only from a personal but a business standpoint. They have an image to protect. Take Kenny Rogers's situation. It was revealed that he used an 800 number for phone sex when a couple of the women he had given his number to went to the media and filed lawsuits. Kenny's personal life suddenly became public.

LORIANNE: Kenny appeared on *Larry King Live* to explain. He said that he and his wife, Marianne, had been having trouble at home. They had separated and had been talking about divorce. With the frightening spread of AIDS and other diseases, he said his way of having safe sex was over the phone. He said these were women to whom he had given his number, they had called it, and now they had filed lawsuits accusing him of sexual harassment. He said they had been willing, he had not harassed them. "They didn't have to call the number," he said. "They could have hung up at any time." Yes, he was humiliated that most of America now knew he was having phone sex while he and his wife were separated. But the only way to put the issue to rest, in his opinion, was to face the public and tell the truth.

CHARLIE: None of that publicity seemed to excessively hurt Kenny. He had enough going on with his career that he was able to survive the negative press. He had the movies and other works to take the public's mind off the sexually oriented reports.

LORIANNE: We are certainly not saying that all the artists are promiscuous. But we do know they have the opportunity. I've heard tales of women who write their home phone number or hotel room number on their bras or panties and toss them on the stage. One of the funniest stories I've heard was told to us by Ricky Van Shelton. He said that he was in the middle of a song, when a pair of panties came flying by and got hung up on one of the knobs on his guitar neck. He kept singing and tried to shake them off, but the panties would not fall off. He said, "What do you do in a situation like that?" Finally, he decided to just let them hang there until he finished the song. Then he removed them. Needless to say, the audience got a huge kick out of it.

CHARLIE: But what about the girls who wait for the artist at the bus after the show? He can't avoid that because the bus is sitting outside the arena. Or they might be waiting at the hotel. They know the hotels the artist will select. They know his itinerary. They track him down. They leave nothing to chance. There doesn't seem to be any limit to what goes on. We've heard stories of artists being delayed for interviews because they were partaking in the back of the bus. Sometimes it is more than one woman. Two or three will get together and go to a concert hoping to tag-team a star.

LORIANNE: Ricky Van Shelton told me of a time before he cleaned up his life when he awoke in his bus in a drunken fog and heard a girl in the sitting lounge yakking away. He said he walked out there and didn't know who she was. He didn't even know her name. He assumed he had picked her up in the bar where he had been the previous night. He couldn't even remember if he had sex with her. So he kicked her off the bus. He never did know what happened. When he told me the story, he looked disgusted with himself for having acted that way.

CHARLIE: My theory is women are attracted to the stars because these guys are looking their best onstage. The hats, the boots, the big belt buckle. They have their own look. The ladies want to be close to them, they want a little glory in their lives, because they know the masses are attracted to these entertainers.

LORIANNE: Maybe one reason a lot of the male artists find it so difficult to turn away all the attention is because so many of them felt very much like outcasts when they were growing up. They channeled their emotions into their songs, and they started singing in the first place because they discovered girls like guys who sing and play the guitar. Many, many stars have told us they were considered geeks in junior high or high school. But when the girls learned they played in a band, something extraordinary happened. I remember when I was in junior high, all the girls wanted to date the boys who played in our school rock band. They wanted to date these guys even more than the football players. Being in the band made them cool, made them popular.

CHARLIE: I wonder if these artists, male or female, would partake on the road if there were not problems at home base? Certainly, there are more opportunities to cheat than there are in a lot of other professions. But a lot of what occurs on the road stems from the relationship back home. Those who are trying to protect their relationships make adjustments to the road life. Some bring the family with them. Others fly to their bookings and fly back so they can spend more quality time at home. We know a lot of artists who make this effort. Tracy Lawrence is a good example. Tracy almost worked himself to the bone in years past. He did something like 285 dates in 1992. In 1993 he trimmed it to about 200.

Then he got married and plans to do less each year and make them count. That's an indication he will modify his career because of his personal life.

LORIANNE: But it's not always easy. I remember the example of Ricky Skaggs when he was a rising star several years ago. Everybody knows that Ricky is devoted to his home life with country star Sharon White. He told us that one of his associates at the time had requested he take his wedding ring off when he was posing for his album cover. He asked, "Why do you want me to do that?" Turns out, they wanted Ricky to present the image of the new "young country hunk." He was told that the female fans will spend more money buying albums and concert tickets if they think the artist is single and available. Supposedly if you sport your wedding ring and come off as a happily married guy, the women are not going to be attracted to you and they won't buy your albums. They wanted to play on Ricky's sexuality. He said, "No. I'm not doing that. I'm not going to pretend I don't have a wife and a family I love in order to sell records." I thought it was refreshing to see him take that stand. Ricky ended up winning the coveted Entertainer of the Year, so he was right in what he believed.

CHARLIE: Some stars take a different approach in deciding how involved their families will be in their careers. For example, certain band members have said that their band has a rule that no wives or families are allowed on tour. The bands that have this rule say that it just gets too complicated and confusing to have so many people on the road at the same time. Point taken. But I often wonder if some of the band members aren't worried that if one or two wives come along and see what the others are doing, they'll go back and tell the other wives. A rule like that is a built-in safety valve.

LORIANNE: In some ways, life on the road leaves artists in a no-win situation. Hank Williams, Jr., has been married a few times and he told me the fight was always the same. He'd come home after a long tour, so happy to sleep in a real bed and eat home cooked meals. But his wives were as home weary as he was road weary. They were ready to get dressed up and go out to dinner, they longed to attend parties. Of course, Hank had had his fill of socializing, so they ended up fighting the whole time he was home about what they were going to do together. Hank admitted that oftentimes he couldn't wait to get back out on the road.

CHARLIE: These pressures aren't new in the music business. A lot of the artists feel that because of the history of this industry they are free to get out there and sow a few wild oats. That is true not only in country music, but in all traveling entertainment shows.

LORIANNE: It's almost as if the newer stars had to relive the legend. Waylon Jennings and Johnny Cash have told us how the legend of Hank Williams influenced them. They thought that being a country music star meant an artist had to work himself to death, had to drink, do drugs, chase women. Of course, Hank Williams didn't do drugs as much as he had a drinking problem. Waylon had a hit song about trying to live the legend: "Are You Sure Hank Done It This Way?" Waylon finally realized that there was something wrong with that lifestyle. I've wondered why Johnny Cash and Waylon Jennings finally did settle down. Maybe Ricky Van Shelton helped answer that question when he was talking about that girl on his bus. He said, "It gets very empty. I remember sitting there, looking at this girl whose name I didn't even know, and wondering, 'Why am I doing this?' It made me feel sad."

You shudder at the chances some of them take. Clint Black had a child from what was apparently a one-night stand with a girl he met at a concert.

CHARLIE: We sat on the story about Clint Black when we first heard about it. I was playing golf with Clint and he asked us, out of respect for the child, to lay low on it until some of the legalities could be worked out. I came back to the office and we all discussed it and that was we did. We eventually had the story on several weeks later.

This is a tough business. I was talking with one fellow who had been a road manager since the 1960s. He had recently retired and started another business. He said, "I got tired of the road life. I couldn't keep up with the pace anymore. It took a toll on me, mentally and physically. If there were problems at home, it was easy to look for a quick fix. Sex on the road is like a drug." Addiction is easy.

LORIANNE: I am often asked how the wives and girlfriends deal with this. There is a lot of denial. Some wives look the other way and don't ask questions. Others have told me they hope and pray their husbands will come to their senses . . . that maybe someday they'll change. Now and then they do. On the other hand, you don't hear as many wild stories about the female artists on the road.

CHARLIE: The women are protected. They are not surrounded by other women. They are surrounded by men who work for them. If a female artist has an encounter on the road, it is on a much more discreet level than anything that happens with a guy. A woman has the same temptations, but her activities are not as blatant. At least not in country music.

In pop music, the women seem to get away with most anything. Madonna has a wild lifestyle, and Cher before her. But they just seemed to sell more albums. In country, if the word spread that a female artist was sleeping around, chances are good she would be rejected by her audience. Yet fans don't seem to reject a male doing the same thing. It's just the way society views the sexes.

LORIANNE: We see the double standard even in our interviews. Charlie Daniels was once on our show talking about how wild it can get on the road. He was a sideman for a long time and he was telling stories about the old days. The audience laughed at his orneriness. But if a woman started talking about the same wild, drunken parties on the road, the audience would be indignant. For some reason, it's funny when a man does it, but in poor taste if a woman does.

I've even found there is a double standard in the way that Charlie and I are received as hosts. Charlie can joke about having a Jack Daniel's after the show. But one year, at Christmas, when Charlie was taking a few days off, I mentioned on the air that I was going home and kicking back with a little Jack Daniel's to watch the TNN Christmas special. The phone lines lit up. All the buttons were blinking. As the show's executive producer, my husband was picking up one call after another. Irate mothers were saying, "My six-year-old daughter idolizes Lorianne. She puts Lorianne on a pedestal. How could Lorianne sit there and say that she drinks whiskey? How can you let your wife do that?" I thought it interesting that when men joke about girls or parties or drinking, the attitude is "boys will be boys."

CHARLIE: Other things happen that prompt the public to react before they know the whole story. I remember when it became common knowledge that Joe Diffie and his wife, Debbie, were having problems. A lot of people had seen their breakup coming. Then it got out that he was dating Davey Allison's widow, Liz. As I've been told, she was not a factor in the breakup of his marriage.

Anyway, Diffie was on our show during the peak of the gossip. He stood in the hallway right before he was to go on the show and said, "Hey, you heard all the Joe Diffie jokes?" I said no. He knows that I hear jokes from everybody. People call me on the phone from Music Row to pass on the latest jokes. But I hadn't heard the jokes about Diffie. So he told me a few he had heard. They were really morbid jokes. Joe would tell one, then laugh, a very uncomfortable, embarrassed laugh. I didn't know what to say. I chose to try to forget them because I like Diffie. He is a good person. His private life was his business. When he told me those jokes I could see he was hurting inside.

I only sensed what a battle he had to be going through. In addition to all this, he has a child with Downs syndrome. There is always a feeling of guilt about a marriage breaking up, but he also had the responsibility of his children. Joe had a good support team around him, but there were aspects he had to deal with alone.

LORIANNE: His marital problems were not sudden. Several years ago, I had planned to do a *Celebrities Offstage* segment with him. Then I got a call from his publicist, saying that he was going to have to cancel. He and his wife were having a hard time and they didn't need cameras in their home right then. Later, Joe confided that he had wanted to do the special, but that he had to try to work things out with Debbie. They did try, but the next time I saw him he told me that he had moved out. He said he felt like the weight of the world had been lifted off his shoulders. He felt the problems were insurmountable and was relieved they were finally going to split.

Well, the next time he came on *Crook and Chase,* he brought Debbie with him. I didn't know what to do or say, so I said nothing (about the two of them). He never said a word to me that day about their relationship. They tried for another year to save their marriage. When I heard that they had definitely decided to divorce, I knew they had really tried.

CHARLIE: I talked to Joe backstage at *Music City Tonight* when he was going through all this. I said, "This talk about you and Liz Allison is pretty much front-page news. We need to ask you about it on the show tonight." He said, "Just ask me. Shoot whatever you want and I'll give you an answer." He went on to say, "Nobody knows the story. Nobody really understands this. Davey Allison's wife has nothing to do with why Debbie and I broke up. People are quick to judge Liz for not waiting what they consider a proper grieving time. No one knows what they will do in the face of death. No one knows what something so traumatic can do until they go through it. We're pulling together and helping each other. It is not a sordid tale. We are two people trying to put our lives back together." Situations like that are hard on us, too. These people are friends of ours. We have watched their careers from the beginning. We have worked closely with them in the presentation of their music on our show. We develop a strong bond with a lot of these professionals. It is upsetting to see people's lives hurt for any reason, and it isn't easy to watch as their personal crises become so public. Of course, that goes with the territory. Fans, particularly country music fans, feel they want to know everything about their favorites. I think there does come a point when the artist's life should not have to be analyzed. If the actions don't affect the fans directly, should they have a right to know? We don't always let the artist know that *we're* aware of the problem.

LORIANNE: A big part of our job is to report what is going on with the country stars both personally and professionally. But drawing the line between being informative and hurtful is often tricky, and many times heart-wrenching for us.

Years ago we did an interview with Johnny Rodriguez. He had gone into rehab to kick his cocaine habit, and he wanted to come clean to his fans on our show. You have to remember that in 1971 when Johnny came to Nashville from Texas, he was barely twenty years old. A year later he was swept into a whirlwind of stardom with the first of eleven number one hits. He got mixed up in some bad habits.

But the piece we did on him was wonderful. It showed Johnny for what we believe he is—a sweet and kind person trying to do the right thing.

Later on, it got back to us that Johnny had faltered. He was back to some of his wild ways. In television today, it would have been perfectly acceptable for us to have done a sensational follow-up piece with scream-ing headlines, "Johnny Rodriguez Falls Off the Wagon!" That kind of thing tends to get big ratings, but we couldn't even consider it. How could we slam-dunk the guy when he was struggling to get on his feet again? It was totally out of the question. We understand that ratings are everything in television, but we decided a long time ago that we don't want them on those terms.

What we did do was try to be of some support. We continued to invite him on the show (and to his great credit, so did Ralph Emery on *Nashville Now*). Backstage at our show, I tried in my friendliest, most nonintrusive way to ask if he was staying clean. Johnny shot me that sheepish grin and admitted that he was backsliding. I remember saying something like "Well, you just behave now" or something similarly stupid sounding. I was attempting to be helpful, but didn't know how to do it without sounding like I was preaching or meddling. I think he got the message that we simply cared about him.

We are still good friends today and he seems healthy and happy. This year he married Willie Nelson's daughter, Lana. He even went to see Willie to ask for her hand in marriage. Can you imagine? Johnny still laughs at the thought of it . . . two such unconventional guys taking part in such a traditional ritual, all in the name of love. These outlaws can be so tender.

CHARLIE: Making the right decision about what to do with the infor-mation we become aware of is one of the toughest things we do. Who do we tell, and why? If we do talk, then who is going to get hurt, and how much? Can it snowball and make someone's life a living hell? Can we justify that? If it isn't business, should we broadcast it to sixty-five million households? We are not watchdogs when it comes to monitoring the personal trials of these artists, yet we become aware of so much.

Personal relationships are tough to keep secret in this business, especially for high-profile people like Troy Aikman and Lorrie Morgan. At the beginning of 1993, Aikman had just won the Super Bowl with the Dallas Cowboys and was voted the Most Valuable Player. Lorrie's career was hot. We did an Easter Seals fund-raising event and I had called and asked that Troy appear on it. Lorianne and I had become acquainted with Troy two years earlier. I also asked if we could get him on *Crook and Chase*. It was during his visit to Nashville that his romance with Lorrie started blooming. That night he was on *Crook and Chase* and this big bouquet of flowers was delivered to the makeup room. We always check flowers delivered to our stars to make sure that there's nothing weird. It's not a case of being nosy, it's being protective. We don't want presents and gifts and cards delivered that may be upsetting in some way to a guest. We let the guests know what we have done when the gifts are presented to them, and they appreciate it.

LORIANNE: So we opened the card to make sure it was nothing inappropriate. The flowers were from Lorrie Morgan. When we saw that, we made sure Troy got them.

CHARLIE: Later in the year, in April, I played in Troy Aikman's celebrity golf tournament in Dallas with all the top NFL quarterbacks. They always start the tournament the night before with a big show. Well, Lorrie was the featured performer at the show. And we later saw them at the Academy of Country Music Awards, escorting one another. They were very cautious to begin with and finally came to the realization there was no way to keep the relationship secret. These were two people in the public eye, who were unattached, and were drawn to one another. They tried to keep it quiet for a while, and did. Then eventually the public found out. (As of this writing, they are no longer dating.)

LORIANNE: Tracy Lawrence received some media attention for his lifestyle. Earlier in his career he was sowing his proverbial wild oats. But not long ago, he told me he was so much happier and more content since marrying Frances. He admitted that he had been wild but had settled down. He said, "It's so much nicer to come home to somebody who I know loves me."

CHARLIE: Clint Black may have gone through something similar. He was a good-looking guy coming out of the chute with hot records. He had a fairly erratic lifestyle in the beginning of his career. It's not that the stories about Clint and Tracy are bad. They were single guys out on the road. But I think they were looking for some sort of stability. I remember Clint calling me one Saturday out of the blue. He told me he was coming into town. Then he said, "I'm bringing my girlfriend with me, too." I said, "Who is she?" He said, "Well, you probably know her. She's an actress. Her name is Lisa Hartman." We had seen her a few months earlier at the ACM show, which he was hosting. They had met each other before at one of his concerts in Houston on New Year's Eve. They obviously hit it off from the beginning.

I think Clint was looking for a way to gain some control over his life. But when Clint and Lisa started dating, everybody said, "This is not going to last." The general opinion was that they would last maybe three or four months. No one thought it would work because she's an actress and he's a singer. But look at the compromises they've made. First of all, Clint had a home in Texas, but made a commitment to go to Los Angeles and operate out of there while she did her work as an actress. She has gone on the road with him. They are inseparable. Because they are two very high-profile people, it is easier for them in some ways. It is not like one is going to be pushed out of the way so a fan can get a picture of the other. The fans are going to want a picture of both of them.

LORIANNE: Generally speaking, the younger country artists are more open about their private lives than artists have been in the past. Take Ricky Van Shelton. He admitted to me that he had extramarital affairs. The reason he confessed was because he was speaking out against alcohol. He had become dependent on beer and wine and he felt that the addiction had changed him as a person and led him down the wrong pathway. So he was blatantly honest about these indiscretions in an effort to convince others not to fall into the alcohol trap.

CHARLIE: Artists like Garth and Ricky Van Shelton go public with what they have done for a reason. I think they are trying to help others. I'm sure there have been countless others who have done similar things, but their actions haven't been revealed to the press . . . yet. There are so many media outlets now, all trying to come up with something on artists.

America is celebrity crazy and the public wants to know everything. So the media has to try to dig up what it can. This also goes back to what we said about the loyalty of the country music fans, and how they want honesty. I think we are looking at a new era of country music. These artists are taking charge of a situation they know could eventually become public anyway, so they are addressing the issue before it gets out of their control. By going public, the artists are nipping the problem in the bud.

LORIANNE: One of the relationships that the public still doesn't have the full scoop on is Dolly Parton's marriage to Carl Dean. Dolly says they have an open marriage, but we're not sure what that means. I've seen and heard all kinds of quotes from Dolly saying that she and Carl Dean allow each other to have friends, but that if either fell in love with someone else, it would hurt. And Dolly says they don't discuss their other friends with one another. Kind of vague, isn't it?

CHARLIE: The particulars of their marriage is one of the top-notch secrets of this business. To me, it is fascinating to the point where, maybe I don't *want* to know what is really going on. Of course, this all could be part of Dolly's overall strategy of creating a mystique. The public knows they don't know everything about Dolly Parton. Keeping a little of the mystery may be one of the reasons that she is a superstar.

LORIANNE: Isn't it interesting that no man has gone to the tabloids saying "I had an affair with Dolly Parton?" If she were really having affairs, I'd think somebody would come forward sooner or later. If it's happening, nobody knows. Even when she talks about her open marriage in interviews, it seems like she is teasing about it. That's what she does about nearly everything. She teases about her boobs (as she calls them), her hair, her nails, the whole image. She's so playful. She has never said, "I'm cheating," or "I'm having affairs."

CHARLIE: We don't know what Dolly and Carl's idea of an open marriage is. It could mean they stay out of each other's way for a while. Carl may want to be left alone to run his construction business and Dolly wants to be left alone to run her businesses. Dolly only gives us a look at the surface. She hasn't provided the details. So I think the country music fans have reserved judgment about that situation.

LORIANNE: Besides, there is something inherently angelic and good about Dolly. I have never heard anything about Dolly hurting other people. She tries to help others. She raises college funds for her hometown of Sevierville, TN. She has created jobs for people with her Dollywood theme park. She speaks highly of other people. She is not thought of as a bad person.

CHARLIE: Being involved in the entertainment business can test you. Think about it. Every day you are thrown together with some of the most talented, attractive, intelligent people in the world. They are charismatic and fun to be around, which is partly the reason they became famous in the first place.

LORIANNE: One of the questions most asked of me is "How do you resist the temptation of getting involved with one of these country hunks?" Fans say, "Every time we see you, you're hugging Billy Ray Cyrus or Clint Black is giving you a kiss or Waylon Jennings is giving you a bear hug. How do you resist?" The truth is, I really do love a lot of the people in the business. But it's not the kind of love that could ever get more physical than a hug or a kiss. That would be wrong. To the stars' credit, I've never felt that I have been propositioned.

CHARLIE: Even if I wasn't married and committed, I wouldn't get involved with a star because of the lifestyle I know exists for an entertainer. I wouldn't and couldn't. I have been around the business long enough to know that kind of relationship is just not for me. I've seen how the industry pulls two people apart. If I were attracted to somebody who was out on the road, I wouldn't be able to see her. I'm always here. I'm not the kind of guy who tours all over the place. I'm a homebody. The difficult part for me would be trying to get on the same wavelength and the same speed as somebody in the business. She would have to be very independent. This business doesn't allow for the kind of personal relationship that I want.

LORIANNE: When I first started in this business, I wasn't married. Some of the stars did make advances. But I never dated one. I never went out with them once because I didn't want anybody to get the impression that I was in this business to date country music stars. I guess I didn't want to look like a groupie. I wanted to be taken seriously and have my work respected. Maybe my view of this goes back to when I was engaged to a baseball player and found out that he had cheated on me just a few months before our wedding.

I have never forgotten the disbelief, the horror of that realization. I wonder if the memory of that incident keeps me on the straight and narrow. I would never want to make anybody else feel the way I did. I probably grieved for two years about that. It was just a horrifying thing to find out that the man who said he loved me and wanted me to be his wife had slept with another woman. If a lot of stars who do cheat realized what kind of hurt they were causing other people, I don't think they would do it.

CHARLIE: Our job is to work with these people, not sleep with them. I don't think I've ever left the show saying, "Boy, I wish I could take that person home with me."

LORIANNE: Not even one?

CHARLIE: Maybe I'd like to take a few out to the car, but not home with me! No, all kidding aside, we have so much respect for the business, and the people in it, the chances of anything happening are off the board. I've been married since I was born. So it's not an issue for me. And that's a relief.

To write about life "on the road again" and not tell a Willie Nelson story would be like describing the flood and not mentioning Noah. As it happens, no one gets more mileage out of a bus—in multiple ways—than the red-haired stranger.

LORIANNE: Waylon Jennings recently told me that Willie Nelson is truly a "free spirit," one of the few he has ever known. I agree. Willie is not a publicity seeker or a media hound, so the times I have interviewed him are few. He is not a mean-spirited person and I have never heard him say an unkind word about anyone, but if he wants to connect with you he will. If he doesn't, forget it. I've experienced both with Willie.

Several years ago, he was playing Starwood just outside of Nashville. I was to interview him on his bus right after the sound check, at about 5 o'clock. Well, 5 o'clock rolled around and no Willie. I was told that some friends of his had shown up backstage and he was talking with them. Friends are important to Willie, so there I stood outside his bus, with cameras waiting.

About an hour later, one of his people told me that Willie was starting his concert at 8 P.M. and he would do the interview right after he left the stage, sometime between 10 and 11 P.M. I was a little peeved at having to wait several more hours, but this is how it is working in television, with celebrities. You do whatever it takes to get the job done. I thought I might as well enjoy the concert.

Problem was, ole "free spirit" Willie doesn't like to watch the clock that closely, especially when he is jamming onstage. He likes to play as long as the audience wants to hear him, which means until he drops. It was after midnight when Willie finally ended the concert, soaked up the last of the cheers and applause, and left the stage. I hurried back to his bus with the camera crew. We set up all the lights and microphones, glad to be finally getting our interview, *seven* hours late!

Guess what? No Willie. One of his people appeared again to tell us that more of his friends had shown up backstage and he was talking and jamming with them. When he finally walked onto the bus it was 2 A.M. and I was dead tired, never mind Willie. After a full evening of concert and socializing, he wasn't much in the mood for an interview, so basically

I got a bunch of yes and no answers. It was hysterical, really. I asked all these long, elaborate, and clever questions to which Willie gave one- and two-word answers.

That night, Willie Nelson taught me the value of learning to ask questions that can't be answered with just a yes or no. Also, I never try to interview him before or after a concert. He is just too consumed by the music, and the fellowship, to enter into the interview mode.

On the other hand, Mr. Nelson can be as charming as anyone I have ever met when he wants to be. A few years later, when he was in trouble with the IRS, he recorded an album—*The IRS Tapes*—to help retire his seventeen-million-dollar debt. There were all sorts of rumors going around about how he had acquired that much debt, and about how much this pressure was ruining his life. Willie wanted to clear up a lot of this talk, so he agreed to do a lengthy interview with me. I think we saw the real Willie in that one as this excerpt will show:

WILLIE: Well, I'm not the best business man in the world. I don't think anybody who writes songs and plays can be. I think it's important that you trust someone to do these things for you.

Here's where the free spirit in Willie reveals itself. He really did trust others, and I mean totally, to take care of the millions he was earning while he was "on the road again." His money ended up in tax shelters that were disallowed by the government, leaving him to pay seventeen million dollars in back taxes and penalties.

WILLIE: I'm not a tax dodger. Since 1983, I had paid eight million dollars in taxes. I feel like I received some bad advice and it cost me a lot of money, but I feel it's not a problem that's insurmountable.

Not insurmountable? Here's a man who owes *seventeen million dollars* and he calmly says he doesn't feel it's insurmountable.

LORIANNE: What does money mean to you?
WILLIE: It's a tool to get something done. That's it. You can't eat it!

(His face is shining with a big smile.) You can't smoke it! (He laughs, obviously making a joke about his well-known fondness for smoking marijuana.) I'd rather have a good garden full of vegetables and maybe a freezer full of good meat in the winter than to have a closet full of hundred-dollar bills.

You have to love the guy. For years he has been a superstar, yet his security doesn't lie in anything that superstardom can provide him. I tell him that his attitude about life's difficulties seems to be an inspiration to his fans. I ask him if he ever inspires himself with the way he handles things.

WILLIE: Well, I'm amazed like everyone else that I get into this much trouble. (Big laugh and, boy, is he charming when he laughs like that.)

LORIANNE: When are you going to stop getting into trouble?

WILLIE: I don't know. I seem to be enjoying it. I don't know, I'm pretty happy with where I'm at. I still have all my fingers left (to play guitar), and whatever talent I have. So I'm not unhappy at all.

I tell him that I admire his optimism.

WILLIE: I like to see the funny side of everything first.

LORIANNE: Now, tell me, what is so funny about being in trouble with the IRS? I've gotta hear this.

WILLIE: Come on. Haven't you had a few laughs over this yourself? (He breaks into that broad grin and begins to laugh.) It's so humorous. Here's a guy from Abbott, Texas, who picked cotton half his life, and now he owes *seventeen million* dollars. (We both burst out laughing.)

LORIANNE: You're right. That's funny.

WILLIE: Yeah. *That* is funny!

The Dressing Room: Unlocked

Every television variety show, in one form or another, is an exercise in crisis management. What the audience sees in the studio and on the screen may not reflect all the preparation—or the panic—that takes place backstage.

We both learned a long time ago that this isn't a business where one size fits all. We try to stay flexible and to be aware at all times that even a veteran performer will probably mutter this quiet prayer before the show: "Please, Lord, don't let me screw up."

There are no rules that we know of except the rule of good manners and even this will get you criticized. We have been faulted by some reporters for visiting with our guests before we go on the air. Why this should be forbidden isn't clear. It isn't exactly the same as a groom seeing the bride in her wedding gown, so we are not violating a superstition. And we are not slipping anyone the answers to a quiz show.

Besides, as someone once said, you can't worry about the monkeys throwing coconuts when the elephants are stampeding.

LORIANNE: We've heard that Johnny Carson, and now David Letterman, made it a point not to have contact with his guests before the show. I guess they both thought it important that the on-the-air meeting and the conversation be fresh and spontaneous. Some of the critics think we give our guests a list of questions so they'll be prepared for anything that might be asked. But that isn't what we do. On occasion, and out of respect, we'll work with a guest when there is a touchy subject to broach, but otherwise we just go backstage to make the artist feel welcome.

CHARLIE: We stop by before every show. We're looking to see what kind of mood the person's in. If somebody has something really heavy on his or her mind, it's important that we know about it before we go out there in front of a live television audience. An uncomfortable artist makes the viewing audience uncomfortable. I'm not totally at ease watching an artist break down and cry. When we're doing the show one of the first things I do is look and see if someone is scared. I look at the lips. If the lips have the slightest quiver, I know the person is fearful. In that situation, we make the mood backstage very light-hearted. For the interview, we try to think of what we call the "icebreaker" and have some fun with the artist first. Then we can get into any kind of serious subject we want to talk about with more ease.

LORIANNE: After George Lindsay was on *Music City Tonight,* not long ago, he said he always enjoyed coming on because he knew he would be okay with the two of us. I asked him what he meant. He said, "Well, I'm not a stand-up comedian. I like to bounce off somebody. When I come on, I know you two will take a back seat and let me bounce my gags off you and I'll have a good appearance." This isn't meant to sound like we're bragging on ourselves. It gives an insight into how we try to provide what the artist needs.

Some people may wonder why we don't go for the jugular. Many other shows that are similar to ours do that. Some even resort to sending out cameramen to hide in the shrubbery and ambush the stars just to get a sound bite and footage of people looking startled, with those deer-in-the-headlight eyes. We're in a position where we could do the same, but that's not our style.

Most of the time, our way works in our favor. Over the years, Lorrie Morgan has had her share of ups and downs. We have always been up front with her, letting her know before a show if we wanted to talk about something touchy. Once, right before a show, she said she felt she had talked enough about her husband, Keith Whitley, and could we skip it that night. She may have been feeling vulnerable. We told her the audience still wanted to hear more, but if she wasn't up to it, fine, no problem. Our respect for her feelings enabled us to build a bridge over the years, to a point where she feels she can call us and offer to deal with sensitive issues on the show.

Recently when the tabloids were loading up with articles on her romance with Troy Aikman, she called and said that she was ready to explode. Lorrie felt the rumors about her love life had become too numerous and too ridiculous. She asked me to bring my cameras to her home for an in-depth, personal, no-holds-barred interview. She said to ask her anything, including the rumors about her friendship with Kenny Rogers. She wanted to separate fact from fiction. I probably don't have to tell you that it isn't every day that a major star calls up to say "come to my house and ask me *anything* about my personal life."

During that interview Lorrie admitted that Troy Aikman was "the love of her life." She had wanted to marry him, but said they both knew all along that it wouldn't work out. Their careers kept them moving in opposite directions. Lorrie also denied that she had an affair with Kenny Rogers. She revealed that he was a very close friend in whom she confided, but she denied that she was the reason that Kenny's marriage to Marianne broke up.

Charlie and I try to build trusting relationships with the stars, where serious conversation like this is comfortable, honest, and open.

It isn't *60 Minutes* with the ticking clock, but we are always working against time. Our routine is the same every night. We start with the makeup and hair about 2:30 P.M. The artists have rehearsed their music by that time, and their dressing rooms are right down the hall from ours. So this is when a lot of the hi, how-are-yous take place. The managers and publicists and record companies have provided us with information and we use that material as a base. Then we try to find out whatever is weird or fun. When we meet in the dressing rooms, Lorianne is usually in curlers. None of us have on makeup yet. It's just a nice little social gathering.

LORIANNE: We try to make our shows spontaneous. When Ricky Skaggs was on one night, we had all sorts of things that we had planned to ask him about, including his radio show and his new album. But somehow, after he came on the set, things got a little silly and we got to talking about underwear.

CHARLIE: He had said during the interview that he wanted to relax more. So I told him to put his feet up on the table and make himself at home. And he did. As he propped back and put his feet up, Lorianne pointed out that he had on weird socks. I then asked him if he had underwear to match, and he went off on a story about his trip to Japan.

LORIANNE: When he arrived there, he realized he had forgotten to pack any underwear. He said that in the better Japanese hotels you walk into the hallway and there's a vending machine that has all kinds of things, like toothbrushes and even underwear. So he said he bought some BVDs from a vending machine, and he was wearing a pair of them that very night.

For the most part, the artists are happy with this spontaneous approach as long as we also get some business done. We never want to sit there and do one interview after another that just blatantly plugs a product. The viewers want to be entertained and they want the conversation to be off the cuff. So do 99 percent of the stars. Most of them will tell us, "God, it was great to talk about something beside my career."

LORIANNE: Some of the sweetest moments take place backstage, before the clock starts racing. One day Doug Stone came in an hour and a half before the show. Some of the artists like to arrive early just to visit. I had done a special with Doug when he talked about his heart problem and how he almost died, and as a result of that show we became fairly close. On this day he was in the green room early and was messing around on his guitar.

Doug had his back to the door while playing some of the songs he had recently written. His publicist, Sharon Allen, was there and Charlie had already sat down to listen. Doug was in the middle of a love song and I sneaked up behind him and put an arm around him. He looked around quickly but he kept on singing and didn't miss a beat. Then he leaned over and put his cheek on mine and he finished singing. The minute he sang the last note, he kissed me lightly on the cheek and asked, "Do you want to hear some more?" We were all in that room for nearly thirty minutes while he was singing some beautiful songs, just Doug and his guitar. We were hearing one hit song after another. I'm sure Doug sits around and sings like that all the time—no big deal. But for us it was an incredible experience. His raw talent filled the room and we almost forgot we had a show to do!

CHARLIE: Speaking of "raw," usually I'm in the back getting the latest jokes from everybody else. These artists pick up some of the trashiest new jokes on the road anyone has ever heard. Some of the world-class joke tellers are Doug, Jimmy Dean, Joe Diffie. Roger Miller was a great joke teller. If I see Jimmy Dean in the hall, he doesn't even say hello. He greets you with a joke. He loved to come in and repeat jokes that President Bush had just told him, maybe a little off-color but not gross. Of course, we'd never tell these jokes on the air.

LORIANNE: When I'm in the hallway and I see Charlie holding court with all the country stars and they're all in a little huddle giggling, I know they are telling jokes. I'll walk up to the middle of this pack of guys and say, "I want to hear them, too." Someone like Joe Diffie will say, "Aw, we can't tell these jokes to a girl." And I say, "Hey, I'm a brazen hussy. Charlie made me this way." Some of them will break down and tell me the joke, but others like Marty Raybon of the group Shenandoah wouldn't tell me one if he was being tortured. I enjoy seeing what reaction I get when I walk up and insist on hearing a joke. It's kind of funny. I guess I'm invading their male bonding ritual!

CHARLIE: The joke telling is done in fun and to relieve some of the tension of going on a live show. Of course, some artists are born relaxed. We were at a concert of Vince Gill's on a late Sunday afternoon, when "Liza Jane" was a big hit. He was so relaxed that ten minutes before he was to go on, he was sitting backstage with us, reading a newspaper, checking the golf scores from the previous day.

LORIANNE: He looked like one of the crew members. He had on a baseball cap and a cup of coffee in one hand. He just sat there, browsing through the paper and sipping his coffee. Vince doesn't have to get himself psyched up for a performance. He is one of those people who can walk onstage and just do it.

CHARLIE: About ten minutes later, Vince was onstage putting on the highest-energy performance anyone has ever seen. He just turned it on, click, and he went through the crowd picking "Liza Jane." It was amazing to see the transformation.

As hard as we try to make things comfortable for our guests, there are always going to be those unavoidable tense moments. We had booked Tammy Wynette on the show when she and her husband were having a problem with the IRS. They were threatening to foreclose on her house.

LORIANNE: Her husband, George Richey, had called me on the phone and told me not to ask Tammy about the house or the IRS. I said, "Well, it's in the news so we need to at least mention it. If Tammy can't talk about it she can simply say so." But Richey was adamant that the subject be off limits.

CHARLIE: The day of the show, Tammy and George were in their dressing room. I went in and said, "How about this house deal?" And before I finished the sentence, George came back with a strong, "No, no, no, no!" It was a very uncomfortable moment because we knew them both well and we weren't ready for that reaction. I guess he was totally frustrated with the situation and the press coverage. I had never seen George like that.

LORIANNE: Then George looked at me and said, "We talked about this and we had an agreement." I didn't know what to say. He really put me against the wall. So we just backed off. He wouldn't even discuss it. We're not telling the story because we think it makes George look bad. He's a wonderful guy. We think it makes him look good because this is how he loves Tammy and how he stands up for her. Tammy was saying, "Honey, it's all right." But he kept saying, "No, no." Tammy was laughing and she laid her hand on his shoulder.

In his defense, he felt he already had an agreement with me. Maybe he felt Charlie was trying to get around it. He wasn't. Charlie was just trying to find a compromise. All he wanted to do was address it. Unfortunately, we're in a business where a lot of interviewers don't seem to have a conscience. We are not going to hit a celebrity out of the blue with something unpleasant. One night right before Billy Ray Cyrus was on our show, one of his publicists said, "Please don't ask Billy Ray about his children out of wedlock." It hurt me that anyone would think that we might pounce on him that way. We do ask questions of artists on the air, but only after we have alerted them and we know how we plan to handle it. It's simply a matter of respect.

I have a special place in my heart for Billy Ray Cyrus, mainly because he has taken some really low hits from many in the industry and the media. Nobody deserves that kind of treatment.

We first met before his debut single "Achy Breaky Heart" was released and caused an outpouring of love from the fans—and a tidal wave of controversy on Music Row. Hank Williams, Jr., was having a party at the Ryman Auditorium, the former home of the Grand Ole Opry, to announce the signing of his new record deal with Capricorn. He had invited me to be there to interview him.

During the party, a nice-looking young man walked up and introduced himself. I didn't catch his name at the time, but he told me that his first record would be out soon. He hoped I would think he was good enough to appear on *Crook and Chase*. The conversation was short, but when he turned to walk away I noticed that he had a very long ponytail hanging down the back of his Indian jacket. Later, I noticed him standing off to the side and taking in the whole event like a wide-eyed kid. He was obviously bursting with excitement at the thought of being a part of the country scene someday.

To be honest, after that night I totally forgot about him. Charlie and I have all kinds of nice-looking, talented musicians who approach us hoping to be on the show. Too many to remember. It wasn't until months later that I realized who I had met that night. My husband's daughter, Wanda, had asked me what I knew about this great new country artist she and her friends were going crazy over, the one who sang, "Achy Breaky Heart."

I still had no idea who she meant. Then one day we were over at her house and she screamed at me excitedly to come see what was on TV. It was the video of "Achy Breaky Heart" and there, dancing on the screen, was the fellow I had talked with briefly at Hank's party. He had been so shy and quiet, I couldn't believe what a confident and charismatic performer he was. I knew we had to have him on the show. Suddenly, *everybody* seemed to be talking about Billy Ray and "Achy Breaky Heart." The song was all over the radio, and people were flocking to the country nightclubs to dance to it.

It took several weeks to get him booked on the show because his life had just turned upside down. I'm sure his manager, a friend of ours, Jack McFadden (who also managed Lorrie Morgan and the late Keith Whitley), was just trying to keep control of his artist's exploding stardom.

Backstage the day of the show, Billy Ray was the same quiet, respectful guy I had met months earlier. But rather than showing the innocent exuberance he did before, his demeanor was more contemplative. I could tell he must be trying to deal with the whirlwind happening around him. I immediately felt respect for the effort he was making to keep his new life and career in perspective. He wanted to do it right.

In the twelve years I have been in the middle of country music, I have seen a lot of stars rise, and rise quickly, but I had never seen anyone soar as quickly as Billy Ray. Perhaps that was why he was the target of so much criticism. He became an instant phenomenon and there wasn't a body of work for the critics to look back on in order to define him.

So here was a guy who came on the scene bursting with sex appeal and a song that was just plain fun. He was immediately labeled as a beefcake poser who lacked substance to his music. Who knows, maybe if he had looked differently he would have been accepted more readily. But the combination of looks, stage presence, and a song that reached out and grabbed the fans was more than some people could handle. The insults started flying. I even remember comments that he was an embarrassment to country music. Excuse me? There are many other artists who record fun songs, who dance onstage, who have muscles and ponytails and can make the girls scream just by raising an eyebrow.

So why was Billy Ray the one being blasted? I do know that when Billy Ray made the scene people couldn't believe he did it without the showcases, the research, the media training, all the usual building blocks an artist has to go through. He did it with one video. Billy Ray broke all the rules, whether he knew it or not, and rather than being happy for him many were miffed. How could a guy sell *nine million* records of his debut album and nobody even saw him coming?

You can see how this could shake up an industry. The argument went take a song like "Achy Breaky Heart" has no substance, and therefore it is bad for country music. The purists have always boasted that this was a musical form that mirrors real life, and I believe that to be true. In my "real life" I get reflective and I am touched by songs that dig deep, such as "How Can I Help You Say Goodbye," "The Walk," and "He Stopped Loving Her Today."

But I, like most people I know, also like to balance the serious parts of life with just plain fun. If there are songs that help us do that, songs like "Great Balls of Fire" or "Liza Jane," what's the harm? I think there is great social value in music that just makes you feel good, or want to dance, or forget your cares for a while. Not everything has to have a message. If a song like "Achy Breaky Heart" touches millions of people, how can you argue with its importance?

Even with all the turmoil, Billy Ray continues to make music that the fans want to buy, and he puts on concerts they want to see. He has proven his sincerity by putting on benefits, and donating a staggering amount of time and money to help others. Most of this is never reported in the press. I find out about it when the fans write and tell me of his good deeds. The guy may not be perfect—few are—but he deserves more credit than he gets.

CHARLIE: From day one, everybody hopes for a song like "Achy Breaky Heart." When it happens so fast and so big, people are always saying, flash in the pan. Goes along with the territory, unfortunately. Ever since he has come onto the scene, Billy Ray had to battle the industry perception of him; was he serious about his music, was he just a backwoods kid who got lucky? I know for a fact he worked hard to get noticed in Nashville. If you look at his other songs, he has a true talent. "Achy Breaky Heart" opened the door for him and the others are what will keep him around.

Another thing about Billy Ray, he believes in southern hospitality. He just bought a farm not too long ago in Williamson County, and, of course, as any entertainer does, he has to change his phone number quite frequently. He is always calling to give us his new number because he wants us to visit him on the farm. He has a place to fish, a place to ride dirt bikes and four-wheelers. He loves being outdoors with his kid. I haven't had a chance to take him up on the invitation, but I will because my son, Dave, and I like to fish. He is just a very open person, very warm, and I think he has put a lot of what the public says behind him. He is just being himself now and that's starting to come across.

Once Billy Ray got to the studio late, or maybe he had been hiding on his bus because he doesn't like to hang out. We hadn't talked yet, so I knocked on his door. He was getting ready, dressing. I said, "I know we've got an AIDS benefit to talk about, but is there anything else? Anything weird going on?" He sat there, thinking, while they applied the TV makeup. I said, "Well, how about your love life? You want to joke around about that?"

I could tell he didn't know what to say. Finally, he said, "Do me a favor. Right now, we can't talk about that." I said, "Why don't you tell me off the record." He said, "No, it will be better if I don't say anything." Then, a few weeks later, he got married. He had had plans at that point, but couldn't tell us about them. We understand those situations. He had to put on a disguise to get his marriage license because he wanted it to be a secret. During the ceremony, he had his ponytail under a baseball cap and he wore sunglasses and added a mustache to disguise himself.

He and his bride, Leticia, went down to the Williamson County Courthouse and the staff there didn't realize who he was until they looked to see who signed the license. Of course, the license said Billy Ray Cyrus. The people who did the paperwork were very protective of him. Their attitude was that if he was going to go to all that effort to hide his celebrity status, they needed to help him out.

LORIANNE: It can be a beehive backstage. Because we visit with the artists before the show, we know what they will and will not talk about. But sometimes there are situations like we had once with Larry Gatlin, when the artist has just come off the road and he's tired and it is all he can do to make an appearance.

Larry is not the kind of guy to hide his feelings, and that's an understatement. Let me preface this story by saying I love Larry Gatlin. One time when he was on our show, I got a frantic knock on my dressing room door. One of our talent coordinators said, "Lorianne, you've got to do something. Larry Gatlin is here and he's upset and I don't know what to do." I walked back to his dressing room. I knew I could tease around with Larry, so I said with mock sarcasm, "What is your problem? What are you complaining about?"

He said, "Honey, I've been on the road. I am so tired, I can barely get around. I've not seen my wife and children for two months. When I get here, I find out that you have me booked in the middle of the show. I would like to be up at the top so I can make my appearance and go on home to eat dinner with my family for the first time in two months."

I said, "You got it." So we went downstairs and we reformatted the show. Then he was fine. Larry kept thanking us. I too have my days when I'm tired and I know that on those days if something isn't right, it will set me off. That's why I asked Larry what was wrong. When he told me and we solved it, everybody was happy. That sort of situation doesn't happen often. Everybody understands Larry. They know he will say what he feels. It's not his style to have just sulked, sat in his room, and stayed upset about the whole show. My attitude is, if artists come to our show and something is wrong, they need to tell us as Larry did, and give us the opportunity to correct it.

CHARLIE: More typically, Larry will come in and ask, "Would you like to see the top of my cowboy boots?" If somebody says yes, he'll drop his pants. I advise people who work on the show not to say they want to see the top of his boots unless they want to see Larry's shorts. He'll drop his pants in front of strangers, stand there, and say, "Aren't these boots pretty?" Of course, if his brother Steve is in the room, he'll roll his eyes and ask, "Am I related to this guy?"

If some artists change under pressure or stress, a rare few undergo a personality transplant between the time you say hello and they appear on the set. These instances are rarely pleasant. We find ourselves engaging in instant therapy, parenting, or damage control.

CHARLIE: We saw a complete personality makeover when Spike Lee, who directed *Malcolm X* and other controversial films, came on the show. When we talked with him backstage we laughed and had a good time. I really liked him. He was cool, very nice. Then when we got him on the set, he took on an attitude.

LORIANNE: Every question I asked, he looked at me as if I was this silly, shallow white woman who couldn't relate to his world, his message. He looked at me as if I was just stupid.

CHARLIE: I'll tell you what happened. When he walked onto the set, the audience started barking at us. They started going "Woof, woof, woof." We didn't know what the hell that was, although we became aware later that it was a standard, hip, fraternal kind of greeting that became identified with *The Arsenio Hall Show*. The word had gotten out that Spike Lee was going to be one of our guests, and we drew a nice crowd from Tennessee State University, a predominantly black university in Nashville. That was fine. But when the audience started woofing at us, we looked at each other and our faces fell. We thought we were being booed—and for the first time.

Maybe half the audience, and nearly all the students, joined in and Spike just turned it on for them. He's a very smart man, a good promoter and a talented director, and he started to playing to the reception. He stopped talking to us like we were fellow human beings.

LORIANNE: It was such a sharp contrast. Before we went on the air, he was almost a shy fellow, gentle, and we were people just making small talk. Then when he went on the air, he became the black avenger promoting his black film. He treated us as though we couldn't possibly understand what he was talking about since we were white, and he tried to make us look foolish. I wasn't angry. I was hurt and puzzled that he felt he had to do that. Here was a man who claimed to be trying to ease the tension of race relations.

CHARLIE: We're not naïve. Sure this is the south. The old redneck image is still out there. But country music crosses every social line you can name. When Charley Pride is on the show, we don't introduce him as a black country singer. We don't say anything about his color. We're professionals and that's the way we try to approach every show and every guest.

In the end, you try to be fair. You make certain allowances for the artistic temperament, for insecurity, and even personal agendas. But one way you can measure the quality of people is how they treat the people they don't think they need. A form of arrogance we can't abide is the guest who treats the two of us with warmth and treats our crew like dirt.

LORIANNE: Every now and then a star comes in and he is peachy keen with Charlie and me because he wants to be sure we have a good rapport for the interview. But he's rude to the crew. One person who did that was Gallagher, the comedian who does the sledge-o-matic act. He was short and biting with the crew. One of our staff, Donna Hughes, was assigned to take care of him during his *Crook and Chase* appearance. She was asking him about his flight and if there was any way she could be helpful. He said to her, "I'm in a bad mood because the flight attendant would not *stop talking to me* (at this point he glared at her), and I don't want to be *talked* to."

She said she was sorry he was having a bad day and asked if she could get him something to drink. He crossed his arms and looked away, as if to say "I'm not going to answer. Can't you take a hint?" He was very difficult backstage. But when he walked on with us, he was the fun-loving Gallagher we had become so familiar with. It makes you think twice about having a guest like this back.

CHARLIE: As a barometer for situations like that, I use Bob Morrison, our stage manager. Bob is always working with artists to ensure that our crew gets the right camera angles, and the band is set up properly, all that sort of thing. If I mention a name and Bob's face turns beet red, I know that person has been ugly or whatever to Bob Morrison. He will do anything to make it easier for the guests to perform at their best. I can tell from his reaction if he has had trouble with an artist, or the band. Sometimes a situation of rudeness gets so difficult that it has to be addressed by the management company. Our staff isn't here to be stepped on. We look out for our crew. We're out front, taking bows for the hard work they put in daily on this show. So because of the way Gallagher treated our crew, it may be a while before we consider having him back.

LORIANNE: I can't be a hypocrite and I won't be two-faced. If someone is rotten to everybody around, I don't want to promote his or her career.

We were proven right about Gallagher. Later, he got into a mess in Las Vegas. According to media reports, he squirted a toddler with a fire extinguisher and scared the child to tears. The audience booed him for that and he started yelling back. Then there was an altercation and he ended up walking off the stage. We don't want to be connected to performers with that mentality. In this day and time, thankfully, there are just a few who have the attitude "I can do anything I want, even if it's immature, because I'm a star and I can get away with it."

As a contrast, we also experience warm and tender moments. The Oak Ridge Boys were on the *Crook and Chase* show just after they won the Group of the Year award at the *TNN Music City News Country Awards*. Quite honestly, it had been a while since they had won anything. They were shocked. Joe Bonsall cried during his acceptance speech.

Before our show, Joe knocked on my door and he came into the dressing room and we talked for the longest time. He poured his heart out about how much winning that award meant to the Oak Ridge Boys. He said, "We're not twenty-year-olds playing in a band anymore. We're not just starting out. But we still have the fire. We get out in a concert and work as hard as anybody." He was proud that they hadn't changed their way of doing things, and that they had been honored and recognized for it.

CHARLIE: All the people who work with them are decent and humble because the Boys are like that. They bend over backward to make things happen, to make them work. They often confide in us. Like most of us, sometimes they just need to talk.

LORIANNE: A few years ago, we were hosting Jamboree in the Hills in Ohio, a wild, four-day live concert. A hundred thousand people showed up for those four days. The Oak Ridge Boys drove up an hour or so before we were to introduce them onstage. While another act was performing, we went backstage to talk to them. Joe cornered us in the back hallway and said, "Duane's mom died this week and we're still in a state of shock."

This was going to be his first appearance since he lost his mother. But instead of all of them being reserved and staying on their bus and being depressed, which they had every right to do, Joe came out to tell us what had happened. We talked about it, then we said, "Hey, let's keep this performance in the family. We'll be the only ones who know, but let's make this concert a celebration for Duane's mother."

I remember, just before we announced them, we were all backstage with our arms around each other, hanging on to each other. It was a highly emotional night. There were no tears. It was like a support system among friends. They went out there and flat swept that concert. The crowd didn't want them to leave. The Oak Ridge Boys always do a great show, but we knew the underlying energy that day was a little something extra for Duane.

CHARLIE: Often, we innocently trigger emotions in artists while they are on the show. John Anderson was on the show one night, and totally unrehearsed, Lorianne wound up dancing with him as the credits rolled at the end of the show.

LORIANNE: John had opened the show with his hit, "Money in the Bank." When he sat down to do the interview with us, I mentioned that many of his songs are good dancing songs. And I asked him if he was much of a dancer. He said, "Are you kidding? I'm probably the world's worst dancer." That's all he would say about the subject on the air.

After the interview, he told Charlie and me the reason he didn't dance. His feelings had been mortally wounded when he was in the seventh grade. He said he always had been real shy and had never learned to dance. But he got up his nerve at a school dance and decided that he was going to go for it. The song was the pop hit "In-a-Gadda-Da-Vida" by Iron Butterfly. He got out on the floor with this girl and he just cut loose. He was going to town, letting out all of his inhibitions. He was dancing! The next thing he knew, the girl turned around and walked off the floor and he never saw her again.

CHARLIE: He said his response when she left him alone on the dance floor was "Well, shit." After that, he never tried to dance again because he had been so mortified by her reaction. Of course, he was laughing his butt off telling the story.

LORIANNE: John thought it was so funny he could barely finish the story. At the end of the show, while the band was playing and the credits were rolling, I went up to him and invited him to slow-dance. And you know what? It was proof that some people have more rhythm in their heart than in their feet!

Tornadoes and Other Things out of the Blue

The television box was never meant to be a kind of polygraph machine, but in the long run it has a similar effect. If you're a phony, if you pretend to be someone you are not, you won't last. You can't fool the viewer night after night. The TV eye will expose you.

For a show to succeed, you have to know what your audience wants, what your role is, how to follow the flight plan and still be able to deal with the unpredictable.

It does bother us when we make mistakes, but we usually go along with Jim Owens, who prefers not to edit them out of the tape on the theory that the viewers enjoy them. As our esteemed producer keeps reminding us, those moments are much more fun and memorable than the ones that we plan. For this reason, our producers sometimes deliberately throw us a curve. In other words, we can't trust anyone! So . . . we're always ready for anything . . . almost.

CHARLIE: There is a segment on our show where we sometimes have a group interview. One night the guests were Pat Boone, Aaron Neville, Bobby Bare, and Chet Atkins. Chet had been feeling ill so he left the stage early. As we began the segment we just started shooting the breeze. Bobby has a store called The Bare Trap across the street from the Opryland complex and he had brought us some of the stuffed bears he sells there. Pat was talking about the fact that he was doing the role of Will Rogers in *The Will Rogers Follies* in Branson. He had brought some ropes so he could demonstrate some rope tricks (and though we didn't know it, he was wearing some "extra hair" to help him look more like the cowboy philosopher). He stood up right there in front of the couch and coffee table and he was doing pretty well. The audience was applauding and cheering after his first demonstration. Then he got another rope that was a little bigger and started twirling it up and down and sideways.

LORIANNE: Now about this time, our stage manager Bob is signaling us to wrap up the segment and introduce Kelly Lang and the band for a performance.

CHARLIE: But Pat was on a roll, so we let him go. He went back and got another rope. He was spinning it and then he stepped inside it and started to bring the rope back up. Well, when he did that, whoof, the rope caught his hair.

LORIANNE: And that "extra hair" flew off his head and went sailing toward the close-up camera.

CHARLIE: We were stunned, but Pat, without hesitation, went right over, picked up the hairpiece, and stuck it back on his head. It was crooked, of course, and he looked at himself in the monitor and started to straighten it. All of this is on camera. While Pat was trying to smooth out his hair I was sitting there with two stuffed bears and all I could think of was to hand one to Pat. Well, he put it on his head.

LORIANNE: We were all laughing. The audience was clapping. Bobby Bare was howling. Even Aaron Neville who is fairly serious was laughing. By then I think Pat's adrenaline must have been going. He was hamming it up and kept moving his hair around. He mentioned it was some hair he'd had made for his role in *The Will Rogers Follies.* Then he reached over and grabbed Aaron Neville's hat and put it on.

CHARLIE: I thought it was a tremendous recovery. But when Pat took Aaron's hat, it worried me. Aaron had had the hat on when he arrived that evening and I hadn't seen him without it. When Pat grabbed the hat, I was thinking, "Oh my God, what if Aaron has See Rock City tattooed on his forehead, or something?" And cowboys and country singers are funny about having their hats touched anyway. But it seemed okay. Pat handled the whole thing like a professional. I have so much respect for him because he kept his poise and humor.

LORIANNE: I kept trying to cut in because I wanted to end what I thought was a very embarrassing moment for Pat, but he kept kidding around. The audience was loving it. Finally, I said jokingly, "It's all right. That happens to Charlie all the time!"

CHARLIE: Let me say here that neither Lorianne nor I wear hairpieces or wigs. However, I was feeling really glad that I had let my wife talk me into those hair transplants the year before. We were trying to move on, but when I looked over at the band they looked like a train wreck. All their instruments were down and the singers were doubled over laughing. Everybody was out of control. I was thinking, "Uh-oh, how can I possibly throw this show to them now?"

LORIANNE: To make matters worse, the song Kelly and the band were about to perform next was "Please Release Me, Let Me Go." When we announced it the audience went to pieces again. Kelly told us after the show that she didn't know how she could keep a straight face and still sing that song after what happened. Somehow we all got through it.

CHARLIE: While Kelly and the band were performing, I followed Pat backstage. I gave him a hug, a kind of laughing embrace, and I said, "Man, you handled that like a champ." He responded, "Wasn't that a scream? I guess I should have glued that thing on but I'm not used to it yet. At least everybody could see I do have hair of my own!" Then he said, "My wife, Shirley, is probably having a heart attack right now." It isn't that Pat is bald, by any means. His hair is thinning some (whose isn't?) and it's understandable why he would want to augment it, especially to play Will Rogers who had such thick Indian hair. He takes great pride in his appearance, anyway.

LORIANNE: I will never forget how calm Pat Boone was about the whole thing. We have a curtain call at the end of the show where all our guests come back out and we thank them in front of the audience. Pat walked right out there. He didn't seem embarrassed at all.

CHARLIE: When the camera went to him, he even did a little flip with his curl in front, like Will Rogers. The audience howled again.

You never know when you will see an example of grace under pressure. Take the show that has became a part of the folklore of Nashville—the night Charlie was "flashed" by Lorrie Morgan. According to a tabloid story, the incident upset Troy Aikman, who was dating Lorrie at the time. It turned out to be a birthday gag on Charlie.

CHARLIE: Lorrie is a big practical joker herself. So the two of them, Lorrie and Lorianne, set me up to think I was doing a satellite interview with Lorrie as a birthday present.

I turned around and there was Lorrie on the big screen in a fur coat. I thought she was off in Canada somewhere. In the middle of the interview she told me to wait for just a minute . . . that she was walking off camera so she could bring something for me to see. Then she walked out, live, on the set, which caught me by surprise. She came out with her back to the audience and cameras, threw open the coat and flashed me, which definitely added to the shock. Eventually, she took off the coat and faced the audience revealing that underneath it she had on a little blue jeans outfit.

But the tabloid mixed up this incident with an earlier one, on my first *Funny Business* show, when Lorrie flashed me and kept her coat *on* because she was wearing a little bikini. That first time, people kept asking me what was under the coat. Finally, I said on the air that she was wearing a little-bitty bikini and there wasn't enough material to blow your nose on. It was interesting that a tabloid would pick up these two incidents from our show. Later, I asked Troy about it and he laughed and said there wasn't any truth about his being upset with me over those reports. He did say he would have preferred that she had done something a bit different.

We don't know which philosopher first spoke the words, but we believe in them: "There are two things you can't do anything about—yesterday and tomorrow." The excitement is in waking up every morning not knowing exactly what to expect for that night's show.

LORIANNE: When we do media interviews, sometimes Charlie jokes that to keep our ratings high our new season of shows will include nudity. He's obviously kidding, but one day it looked like it was going to happen. The *Crook and Chase* show hadn't been on the air all that long when Lee Greenwood came on. We had mentioned in several of our reports that toward the end of his concerts, Lee gets so pumped up he starts peeling off his clothes. First, he takes off his jacket, then his shirt, and soon he is singing in his jeans and boots. He was scheduled to appear live on our show and he decided to have a little fun with us. He said, "Your reports leave the impression that I take off my clothes all the time, but that's not true." Then he got up and pulled off his shoes and socks and threw them across the stage. Then he shed his jacket and pulled off his shirt. By this time, I was scared half silly. Then he dropped his pants and I was in such shock that it took me a minute to realize that he was wearing a basketball uniform!

He turned and said, "Hey, if you're going to report that I take my clothes off, then let me take 'em off!" The crowd thought it was hilarious.

CHARLIE: I knew he was going to do it, but Lorianne didn't. Lee had on a Harlem Globetrotter uniform under his clothes. The fans know that some of the country music artists will do almost anything to get the best of us, and they like that. The first thing that crossed my mind that night was if Lee takes off his shoes and socks, does that mean I have to take off mine? I was trying to remember if I had a hole in my sock. The last thing I wanted was to yank off my shoe and have my big toe sticking out. But, fortunately, I didn't have a hole in my sock.

LORIANNE: So much of what happens on the show is spur of the moment. We usually don't know what the artists are going to do or say. One night Martina McBride told a John Bobbitt joke. (Bobbitt became famous after his unhappy wife, Lorena, amputated his manhood with a kitchen knife. Doctors later reattached the organ in One of the Great Moments in Modern Medicine.)

CHARLIE: Here was cute, petite Martina McBride sitting on the sofa on *Music City Tonight,* such an unlikely person, telling a Bobbitt joke. Nobody could believe it. She started off by saying she was going to do some writing with John Bobbitt. Not knowing where she was going with this, we said, "Oh, really? Tell us about it." She said, "Yeah, he already wrote that one big hit with George Strait entitled "I'd Like to Have That One Back.' " She just laughed and the audience got a big kick out of it. Some of our stagehands asked me later if I thought she had tarnished her image at all by telling that joke. I said I didn't think so. Actually, she may have pleasantly surprised a few people.

LORIANNE: As you know, Charlie loves a good joke, but he did have to step in one night and put a halt to Williams and Ree before they went too far.

CHARLIE: They were telling another John Bobbitt joke. I thought I had an idea of what was going to be said. Terry started off with "Do you know what they would have charged Lorena Bobbitt with if she had missed?" I stopped them right there and changed the subject. The punch line was "If she had taken the knife and missed, she would have been charged with a simple missed-a-weiner." We couldn't let that on the air.

You have to draw the line somewhere, but you make a lot of allowance for talent and even more for genius. As a rule, country music fans feel closer to their legends because in most cases they have lived their songs. Superstars like Merle Haggard are so loved because they are truly in touch with life's emotions and can convey them flawlessly in their music.

LORIANNE: One afternoon we sent a limousine to pick up Merle Haggard, who had been booked on our show several months before. The limo driver called about thirty minutes before show time and said he had been waiting and waiting, but he couldn't find Merle. He said he had knocked on his hotel door, but there was no answer. So, finally, someone who worked with Merle went over to the hotel, got into the room, and found him sound asleep. Merle literally dragged himself out of bed, put on some clothes, borrowed a hat, and climbed into the limo. He didn't have time to shower, brush his teeth, or comb his hair.

CHARLIE: He came on the show wearing a dirty old John Deere baseball cap. He sang an old army song entitled "Only Me and Old Soldiers Give a Damn." He sat there and talked real slow, and the crowd was with him. Their attitude seemed to be, it's Merle. He's a legend, an icon, and we don't care what he did or what he is doing.

LORIANNE: I'm sure he was in such a sleepy fog that he barely remembers that appearance. But when you think about it, how many stars would have actually gotten out of bed to come do the show? Most would have apologized and canceled, but Merle knew the audience was waiting to see him and he came right on over. He has a lot of hard miles on him, but he is still a cool guy.

Not everyone is as obliging as Merle, and you have to make a decision when people are rude or difficult on the air. Do you pretend not to notice, or do you confront them? As the hosts, you try to be diplomatic, but frankly it isn't a job where you should be passive.

LORIANNE: A troubling moment for me was when the actress Julie Harris appeared on the show. She was touring in the stage production of *Driving Miss Daisy*. We sent out a crew to shoot part of a scene so we could show a clip during our interview. In my introduction of the clip I said, "Julie plays a southern belle." At that point, she interrupted me and said, "I do *not* play a southern belle. The woman I play is anything but stupid and frivolous. She is a strong woman who knows what she wants out of life." Clearly, she considered being described as a southern belle insulting.

We went on and finished the interview. During the break, when she was getting ready to leave, I said, "Ms. Harris, just so you know, in the south the term "southern belle" is not derogatory. Southern belles are generally strong, smart women who can take care of themselves." She just looked at me and said nothing.

CHARLIE: Sometimes, the so-called serious actors who come in from New York or Los Angeles and other places have the impression that this is a rinky-dink show because it is not done in New York or Los Angeles. That attitude really irritates us. Between us, Lorianne and I have been in broadcasting for more than forty years. We know our audience. Sometimes the guests do not, and they should rely on us to help them. If they don't, they're shooting themselves in the foot.

LORIANNE: For me, it was a split-second decision. I asked myself, "Do I stand up for myself during the show or wait till we're off the air?" I didn't know which way to go. On the one hand, I didn't want the viewers to think I was argumentative. But I didn't want them to think I had no spine either, and would let an artist push me around. It is a very fine line, how to react to those situations.

Al Capone, you know . . . that famous Chicago philosopher back in the Roaring Twenties, once said, "You can get just as much with a kind word and a gun as you can with a kind word alone." We've done fairly well sticking to kind words, as this story illustrates:

LORIANNE: Several years ago, in the days of the *Crook and Chase* show, our producer took a call from a relative of Lily Tomlin's mother. This person told us that the mother of the actress-comic, Lily Mae, lived in the Nashville area and she had gotten hooked on our show. The caller said that Lily Mae would be really thrilled if we were to say happy birthday to her on the air. We did some checking and found out the request was legitimate. So we gladly wished a happy birthday to Lily Mae. In fact, we do it every year.

Early in 1995, we found out that Lily Tomlin would be in Nashville, not only to visit her mom, but to promote her book, *The Upside Down*

LEFT: *Lighting up the forty-foot jukebox at the grand opening of Country Star Restaurant in Hollywood:* (left to right) *Lorianne, Wynonna, Reba, Vince, Charlie, Peter Feinstein, and Robert Schuster of Country Star Restaurants, Inc.*

RON WOLFSON/COUNTRY STAR RESTAURANTS INC.

RIGHT: *1988. Celebrating Keith Whitley's #1 record, "Don't Close Your Eyes." Lorrie Morgan and Keith were struggling with his alchoholism, so that's sparkling cider in the bottle.*
COPYRIGHT © 1988 DON PUTNAM

LEFT: *This outlaw wormed his way into my heart the first time we met. I've never had a bad time with Hank Williams, Jr.*
JIM OWENS & ASSOCIATES, INC.

LEFT: *1990. When Roy Rogers asked me if I wanted to ride, I thought surely he meant on a horse. Motorcycle riding with the King of the Cowboys was the ultimate experience. Dig the cowboy hat instead of a helmet!*

ABOVE AND RIGHT: *1993. Now you know why I say Waylon Jennings has the best lips in country music. He knocked me off my feet at Jamboree in the Hills!*
JIM OWENS & ASSOCIATES, INC.

LEFT: *As kids, we considered him a big star on* Bonanza, *but we managed to act really cool during the interview! Michael Landon was very serious about producing good TV shows.*
JIM OWENS & ASSOCIATES, INC.

BELOW: *Of all the stars who plotted a return to a "Funny Business" practical joke, my good friends the Oak Ridge Boys were the only ones who were successful. They really got me!*
COPYRIGHT © 1992 ALAN L. MAYOR

ABOVE: *At home with George and his wife, Nancy. George warns me not to ask questions that are too personal. Of course, I did anyway!*
LAURIE LARSON/JIM OWENS & ASSOCIATES, INC.

RIGHT: *1992. Buddies forever. Vince Gill takes time out from one of his heart-melting ballads to spin me around the stage at Jamboree in the Hills, St. Clairsville, Ohio.*
PATRICIA GALLAGHER

LEFT: *Buddy Ebsen shows off his brand of "line dancing"—or "hoofing" as it was referred to in his Vaudeville days.*
COPYRIGHT © 1994 ALAN L. MAYOR

BELOW: *When we welcomed 1993 Super Bowl MVP Troy Aikman, Billy Ray Cyrus* (left) *made a surprise appearance, presenting Aikman with a check for the star quarterback's Children's Foundation. In return, Aikman auto-graphed Cyrus's Cowboys jersey for a St. Jude's auction.*
KAT MILLER/JIM OWENS & ASSOCIATES, INC.

ABOVE: *1994. Just before Christmas, Garth played Santa Claus and presented us with our own copies of his 11 million–selling album,* No Fences.
COPYRIGHT © 1994 ALAN L. MAYOR

RIGHT: *"Mr. Television," Milton Berle made history as he sang on TV for the first time in forty years on our show. Uncle Miltie is joined by his wife, Lorna.*
COPYRIGHT © 1995 ALAN L. MAYOR

L E F T : *Jimmy Dean is the craziest guy we've ever known . . . but has the warmest heart. He's a true friend who will do anything for you.*
JIM OWENS & ASSOCIATES, INC.

B E L O W : *What a thrill for us to partake in a night of surprises for Reba McEntire as we reunite the "entire" family for the first time on live TV. That's Reba's sister Alice Foran seated on the couch (inset)*
COPYRIGHT © 1994 ALAN L. MAYOR

LEFT: *Thumbs-up with Rush Limbaugh in 1993 on his home base*

JIM OWENS & ASSOCIATES, INC.

RIGHT: *With Tony Bennett in New York City. We broadcast live for a week in 1993 from Rockefeller Center.*

KAT MILLER/JIM OWENS & ASSOCIATES, INC.

LEFT: 1992. *We hosted the Hollywood Women's Press Club's 52nd Annual Golden Apple Awards at the Beverly Hilton Hotel. Walter Matthau was on hand to present the prestigous Louella Parsons Award to his buddy Jack Lemmon.*

FRANK TRAPPER

Wisdom of Edith Ann, written in the voice of her inquisitive, little girl character. Our producers called Lily's management and told them we were interested in having her on to promote the book. Of course, they threw in the fact that her mom was a big fan of our show, which had now evolved into *Music City Tonight.*

Lily asked for a tape of the new show, obviously to see if she would feel comfortable appearing on it. A few days later, we got the call saying that Lily would gladly make a guest appearance.

I don't see how you could not like Lily Tomlin. She was both businesslike and matter-of-fact, yet in everything she said and did a real brilliance came through. Responding to the whims of our audience, she effortlessly glided in and out of her famous Edith Ann and Ernestine characters. Quite honestly, I have seen some Hollywood stars who try to take control of a show and leave the host in the dust. But Lily seemed very clued in to what our show was about, what made the audience laugh, and what we as hosts (Rex Allen, Jr., was filling in for Charlie that night) were trying to accomplish. I appreciated her not making us struggle to keep the show on track during her segments. I think the audience picks up on these unspoken moves as well, and they just fell in love with her.

Prior to the show, she had agreed to do an audience participation bit. The fans asked questions of her characters, and she answered as Edith Ann or Ernestine. Lily seemed to enjoy it because she got to do some "improv," and our audience clearly got a kick out of interacting with a movie star.

It's a fact of life for every television host . . . you are not going to connect with every guest. There will be awkward moments or entire interviews that just don't click. Many times we are already in the middle of the interview before we know if there is a good rapport. It's a real high when someone you're not sure of turns out to be a great guest. Such was the case with Tammy Faye Bakker.

Tammy Faye came on the show during the height of the controversy over her husband, Jim's relationship with Jessica Hahn. Keep in mind that at this time nearly every media outlet was hounding Tammy Faye for an interview.

Photographers stalked her. She had gone into hiding and was talking with no one. So imagine our surprise one Monday morning when we found a recorded message from Tammy Faye herself on our office answering machine!

CHARLIE: Tammy Faye was visiting friends in Nashville and actually asked to be a guest on our show. When she arrived she had on all of her much heralded cosmetics. She certainly didn't need any extra TV makeup—she was ready to go on the air. We had some time backstage to welcome her to the show. She was a bit smaller than I thought, very, very petite. If she is five feet tall I'd be surprised.

She had on her spike heels and a little jumpsuit. We were having the kind of casual visit we often do, then Tammy Faye got down to the basics in a heartbeat. I will never forget that directness. She said, "Look, you ask me about Jessica Hahn and Jim and I'll just get up and walk off." She said what happened between them was a fifteen-minute affair, a onetime thing. She said, "It's over with and as far as I'm concerned, it's history. Everybody knows about it, so there's no reason to discuss it further."

LORIANNE: It was odd the way she said it. She had the biggest smile on her face and in her baby doll voice she said, "Now, if you ask me about that I'll just get up and leave." It wasn't said in a threatening tone, but we knew she meant it. Tammy Faye told us she had been watching our show and felt she needed that kind of fun in her life. She also said she wanted to let people know that she was doing okay . . . that she was surviving and working through her personal problems. Most of all, though, she wanted to come on the show and share some laughs again. Charlie had some big-time fun with her.

CHARLIE: I told her that I had seen these T-shirts that had makeup smeared all over the front of them, and read "I ran into Tammy Faye at the mall." So I asked her about the shirts. She had fun with that. Her response was "Well, if they had really run into me at the mall, there would be a whole lot more makeup on the shirt than that!" She was an interesting study in personality. She was delightful. Our crowd got a kick out of seeing her. I don't know whether they agreed or disagreed with what happened in her personal life but they did applaud her and they laughed with her in the interview. She has a very bold attitude about herself.

LORIANNE: She told all kind of stories about going to Kmart and buying hair coloring. She said that one time she used too many hair products at once and ended up looking like a skunk with weird stripes in her hair. She talked about how she can't go to the makeup counter at Kmart without a photographer following her. What I liked about her was that while she is obviously different, she makes no apologies for being that way. Her attitude is, if she wants her eyelashes looking like tarantulas, then that is the way it's going to be. She'll laugh about it, but she's not going to change.

Tammy Faye divorced Jim Bakker while the televangelist was in prison and has since remarried. We hope she's happy. We try not to take advantage of our guests, or make cheap jokes about their problems. If there is any fun poking to be done, we make sure it's not hurtful.

No matter how hard you try to avoid it, you will hurt someone's feelings. You may not know exactly why, but if you stay in this business long enough toes will get stepped on, people will be upset, and you will wake up the next morning feeling like a poached egg.

LORIANNE: I still don't know what to make of what happened between me and Anita Bryant, in January 1990. She had been out of the mainstream media for a while, at least partly the result of the furor surrounding her public disapproval of homosexuals. Anita had been booked on the show to discuss some projects she was working on in Nashville. Charlie and I had asked our bookers to let her know that we felt we had to ask her at least a question or two about the controversy. Was it behind her? How had it affected her life and career? Ours is not the type of show where we routinely leap into sensational issues, but we could hardly ignore something so closely identified with a guest.

The word we got back was that Anita was fine with a few questions, but preferred that we not dwell on it the entire interview. We thought everything was set.

The day of the appearance all seemed well. We met Anita backstage in the makeup area. She was pleasant and comfortable to be around.

Charlie and I told her some of the topics we wanted to hit during the interview. We did not mention the controversy. We didn't want to give her the impression that it was the main topic on our mind, which it wasn't. We were satisfied with the understanding already in place.

To my shock, things turned out very badly. The interview went fine at first, as we talked about some of her past career accomplishments, and some of the new projects she was planning in Nashville. Then, toward the end, I asked how she had dealt with the controversy over her past public statements on the gay lifestyle. You should have seen her face! Her eyes iced over and she looked at me as though I were the lowest insect on earth. We were in front of a live studio audience, so she kept her composure and answered the questions. To this day, I can't remember a word she said. My mind was racing, trying to figure out what had gone wrong.

We wrapped up the interview a few minutes later. Anita greeted the audience and answered their questions and was really quite charming and witty considering that she must have been about to explode inside. She shook my hand and thanked us for having her on the show, but when she turned from the audience her face changed to a look of utter disbelief. I still had no clue as to what was going on. Charlie and I had to finish the show and it was one of the hardest things I've ever had to do.

I wanted to follow Anita back to the dressing room to find out what had just passed between us. I found out from our talent coordinators that after the show, Anita and her entourage walked quickly to her dressing room and closed the door. Apparently, they were inside for quite a while before they left the building. The word was they were *not* happy.

The next morning I called her manager. I couldn't believe what he was telling me: that Anita had had no idea her past tempest was going to be brought up. She felt I had dealt her a low blow and must be trying to make a name for myself as another Geraldo Rivera or Phil Donahue. She thought I had met her in the makeup room prior to the show to be nice and sweet and get her guard down, so I could pounce on her during the interview and get a sensational reaction.

I was speechless. Charlie and I admit that we have made mistakes, like all broadcasters, but we have never had a reputation for being dishonest or deceitful. I explained that we thought we had been cleared by Anita herself to ask the question. I repeated the entire scenario and he was kind enough to say he believed me. He gave me her home phone number.

Now I had to explain it to Anita. I rarely have been so apprehensive in my life. Was she going to scream at me? Hang up on me? When the answering machine answered I must say I was relieved. I left a message telling her that I was deeply concerned that she was upset, and that I wanted to tell her my side of the story.

She called back within the hour. I could tell Anita was a bit wary because she didn't know what kind of story I was going to hand her. I just told her as honestly as I could how the mixup had occurred. I could feel her warming up. In fact, she told me she was sensitive because so many members of the press had ambushed her and she hadn't expected it from me. Gently, I corrected her: It wasn't an ambush. We thought we had had her permission. She said she didn't remember agreeing to that line of questioning.

To this day, I am unsure about what really happened. Was it a mistake by our talent bookers, or did Anita forget? I guess the important thing is that Anita was gracious enough to believe my story. She thanked me for calling because, she said, no member of the media had ever called to apologize to her for anything. A few months later, she invited me and my husband to her wedding.

There was still one more twist to the story. Not long after our interview with Anita, the local morning newspaper ran a front-page article about Anita, in which she offered two pages of opinions, past and present, on homosexuals. I couldn't believe it. She was so distressed by my one question, yet here was this in-depth article on the same topic. At first, I was a trifle miffed that she had made me feel so guilty, when she very freely answered a barrage of questions for the paper. Then I had to remember that she accepted my apology for the misunderstanding and had been kind when she didn't have to be. I just let it go and decided to accept my lesson, which is: If I am to raise a touchy subject, I *always* try to see the artists in person before the interview to make sure they understand how and why it will be addressed. This often creates a bond of trust, which makes for a better interview, anyway.

CHARLIE: One of my lasting embarrassments was when Precious Moments—my nickname for Lorianne, a term of endearment—did a show celebrating my twenty-fifth year in broadcasting. I'm really uneasy about accepting praise. She brought in my high school English teacher, Mae Brooks, who had such an influence on me doing things correctly. That's *Miz* Brooks. She brought in Mavis Livingston, who worked at the radio station in Rogersville and was like a second mom to me. She brought in the first star I ever interviewed, Jeannie C. Riley. Then, at the end of the show, Crystal Gayle came on and brought a gift that Lorianne and the staff had purchased to commemorate my twenty-fifth anniversary. It could not have been a higher compliment, but it was embarrassing because I don't take compliments well.

LORIANNE: Oh, he was squirming. We walked out to open the show and I immediately took over. He didn't know what was going on. His eyes started cutting back and forth, side to side, like "What is this? What's going on?" Then he realized that the whole show was dedicated to him. I had the most fun watching him react because he didn't have a clue as to what was going on. Charlie is the type who likes to be prepared for a situation. He didn't know what was coming up or who was coming out. The entire time he was saying, "What's next? Come on, tell me." I just smiled and kept the surprises coming.

CHARLIE: The problem with being on the hot seat is the fact that you're the only one in the studio who isn't clued in. But it doesn't take much to break up an audience, especially when they expect things to go a certain way. Like the night Lorianne walked out in shoes of two different colors.

LORIANNE: I had on one brown shoe and one black. I guess the dressing room was a little dark that day. Sometimes when I'm in a hurry, I just stick my feet in my shoes and dash off. We were probably about ten minutes into the show when I realized that I had on different-colored shoes. We were interviewing someone and I looked down and shrieked,

"Oh my God!" Charlie reacted as if I had seen a mouse. He said, "What's wrong?" And I said, "I've got on a brown shoe and one black shoe." Charlie immediately had the cameras get a close-up. That happened ten years ago and I still get letters about it."

You can toss vanity out the window, and sometimes the script, when those moments occur that people won't let you forget. And sometimes Mother Nature gets into the act. We hate to be the ones to destroy any illusions, but contrary to the oldest saying in the business, the show doesn't always go on.

CHARLIE: Very high on our list of memories is the time four years ago when our studio was hit by a small tornado. At about one o'clock in the afternoon, Lorianne was in her dressing room, which is adjacent to mine, and I was on the phone talking with my wife, Karen. The whole building started shaking. I said, "Oh damn," and that was the last thing Karen heard before the phone went dead. She was a wreck because she had no idea what had happened.

I came out of my dressing room and Lorianne ran out of hers. We stood there in the hallway and she said, "What's going on?" I said, "I think it's a tornado. Let's get out of here." I grabbed her hand and we headed for the door. All the emergency lights in the building were flickering and we were running through the halls.

This was happening an hour and a half before show time. As we raced around the corner of the hallway we looked out the window and saw the roof flying off the building and sailing down the alley. We kept running. A torrential rain was coming down and the building was leaking everywhere because the roof had been torn off. In no time we had reached a safe portion of the building.

I had my portable phone, so I called Karen and let her know I was okay. About that time the fire department, the police, the utility companies, everybody had descended on the area. Other buildings on the block were damaged. All the windows of a car dealership across the street from us were blown out. Obviously, we couldn't do the show that night. We didn't have any power. Everyone was rattled.

LORIANNE: We called Ralph Emery and asked him to please announce on TNN what had happened. So during his show, Ralph mentioned that nobody should panic but that *Crook and Chase* wasn't going to air live that night because a small tornado had hit their building. He told the viewers our power was out and while we were unable to do the show, everyone was safe. Ralph really helped us out.

There was one priceless moment right after the worst of it happened. Charlie Daniels was scheduled to be our guest, and he got there about forty minutes after the tornado had hit. There were four cars in our parking lot that had been pancaked when the utility poles fell down and smashed them.

So Charlie Daniels came walking up, with his fiddle in hand, inspecting the damage, his eyes big as saucers. The expression on his face said "Holy smoke, what's going on here? I hope they don't blame this on me, I just got here."

To Absent Friends

Death is not a subject that most of us want to get cozy with. We tend not to handle it routinely or gracefully or with detachment.

When a public figure dies, especially one who has entertained us, who has been a part of our lives, there is an added factor. Do we express our grief in private or in public? We mourn as we pray, each in our own way. Tributes can be a sticky thing; they can also be a sincere, and necessary, part of the healing.

In the last decade, country music has lost some of its brightest and most enduring names. There is no ideal time to get sentimental, but we want to mention a few artists who touched us directly. Their deaths were not just a loss to music, but a loss to the living, even to the many who never met them. From our standpoint, we knew them as fans, as friends, as reporters.

Some, like Roy Acuff, died at the end of a long and abundant life and career. In the quality that truly counted—in being truly alive to the joys of the world—he was eternally young.

CHARLIE: The picture that remains the most vivid in my mind is the night they dedicated the Opry House. President Nixon had flown in for the event and he went onstage with Roy Acuff to join him in spinning a yo-yo. Mr. Acuff was so proud of that. He had autographed pictures, all kinds of mementos of that visit. He was so proud of that new building and so proud that he shared the Opry stage with the president of the United States. That was a warm moment.

LORIANNE: I did an interview with him at his house when he was almost eighty years old. That was a few years before he died. After we finished, he said he had enjoyed the interview because I had asked all sorts of questions he had never been asked before. We must have bonded in a special way because after that he would often invite me to drop by for a visit. The Opry folks felt he was such a legend, they had built a house for him on the Opryland complex, where they could look after him. Opryland had been his residence since his wife died. He was very lonely after she passed away and he didn't want to go back to an empty home.

A lot of my personal memories of Roy are connected to that house. His favorite thing was to sit in his big armchair with a huge bowl of M&Ms on the coffee table. I would sit on the couch beside him, and as he talked, he would pick out a handful of M&Ms for me. Then he would get some for himself. We'd sit there popping M&Ms and talk about everything. He loved to reminisce about his performances twenty, thirty, forty, fifty years ago. One reason he liked living in the park was that he could visit with his fans. Mr. Acuff would sit in his rocking chair out on the front porch. People would stroll by and say "howdy" and stop and shake his hand. He just loved that. He was very proud of the park, and of his home.

CHARLIE: Everybody loved Mr. Acuff. If you tried to get into his dressing room on Friday or Saturday night at the Opry, there was a waiting list. It was like trying to get into a hot restaurant. His dressing room door was always wide open. He loved having company. Sometimes he didn't know who many of the people were, but he enjoyed having them. I visited him one night with our camera crew. We were doing some little *Funny Business* segments. I said, "Mr. Acuff, I'd like you to tell me the latest joke you've heard—that we can use on television." He said, "I don't know if I can repeat one or not." He looked over at his longtime sideman Brother Oswald, who was sitting next to him, and said, "Os, what was that joke I heard last week?"

Os went over and whispered a few things in his ear and Mr. Acuff said, "Yeah, that's the way it was." And he started into the joke and said, "Now, what's the next line, Os?" And Os would tell him. Then Mr. Acuff said, "Oh yeah." He told a little more of the joke. The punch line didn't have the same impact but it was hilarious to watch him try to tell it.

He had such a sweet personality, and it was there until the end, in spite of the pain he endured in the latter years. It got to a point where he had to be assisted onto the Grand Ole Opry stage and he sat on a stool. But, boy, he could still sing "The Wabash Cannonball" and "The Great Speckled Bird." It is a treasured memory for those who got a chance to see him do those songs on the Opry. This man was a walking history book. He had started back in the 1930s and 1940s, when country music stars traveled to a show and made five dollars a night. That's hard to imagine these days.

Lorianne: His last year or so, Mr. Acuff would sometimes become despondent about his health. He had developed cataracts, so he had a hard time seeing. There were days when he said his whole body hurt. Once, I saw him walk down the hall backstage at the Opry and as he passed me I said, "Hey, Roy, how you doing?" He just mumbled and kept walking. I knew something was wrong because he was normally so friendly.

I followed him back to his dressing room and asked if he was okay. He knew his health was failing. He didn't talk in a poor, pitiful-me way. He was very matter-of-fact about it. He said, "Sometimes living just gets so hard I think I'm ready to die." A stricken look must have flashed across my face because, very quickly, he added, "I don't want anybody to grieve for me because I've had a wonderful life. I've been able to do everything I've wanted to do. I've loved country music and country music has loved me back." He was very comfortable about having traveled his road, and that it was time to go.

CHARLIE: He had gotten everything in order. His will was done and he had made the arrangements for his own funeral. He took care of his own affairs. He didn't want to bother anybody and he didn't want any hoopla.

Roy Acuff's loss saddened us all, but he left behind a sense of fulfillment. It was nothing like the shock of learning that Keith Whitley was dead as he neared the prime of his career. It was unbearably sad.

LORIANNE: To me it seemed Keith wanted to find the fun and joy in every moment. Charlie, Keith, and I had such a good time any time we were together. I will never forget the day we heard the news of his death. When I got to the studio, Charlie told me to sit down. Then he sat beside me and told me that Keith Whitley was dead. I remember feeling like I couldn't breathe. I wasn't aware that he had been losing his battle with alcoholism. I had heard that he had overcome an early life of hard living.

CHARLIE: After hearing of Keith's death we immediately started to revamp the show. The first reports were that Keith had apparently taken his own life. I thought he must have shot himself. As we learned the details of what happened, we realized that his drinking problem was a deadly one. He couldn't beat it. Lorrie (his wife, Lorrie Morgan) had gone on the road. Apparently, he was by himself and had gotten drunk not on whiskey, but on pure grain alcohol. Then he drowned in his own vomit. It was such a tragic death. Only a short time before, he had been out on his tour bus, celebrating his record "Don't Close Your Eyes" going to number one.

I thought Keith had stopped because he wasn't drinking the day he celebrated the success of his record. He toured Music Row, stopping at key points and having little impromptu gatherings that lasted maybe ten or fifteen minutes. Champagne was being served to the guests, but he said he was drinking sparkling apple cider. I was suspicious and said, "Yeah, right." So I took his glass and took a little sip and I realized he was telling the truth. It *was* apple cider.

We were standing right in front of the building where we taped our show. We still have that picture. Lorrie Morgan was with him. We were all in one big, long line, hugging each other, congratulating him.

A short time later, he was dead from an alcohol overdose. It was so hard to believe. We were in shock. On the day he died, we taped a tribute as part of the show. The next day we went to the funeral home where Keith's body had been taken. Lorianne and I went together. We wanted each other for mutual support because we didn't know what to expect. We didn't know how we were going to react or who was going to be there. It was still early in the morning, a little after ten.

LORIANNE: It was strange when we reached the funeral home. There were fans already gathered out front. When we walked in there was a small room to the left of the foyer that was set aside for family members. I saw Lorrie sitting with her back to the door. I recognized her, even from the back. Her hair was very short and very blond. About that time, I saw her raise a cigarette her lips. Her hand was shaking so badly that she could barely light it.

We went in and we hugged. I remember choking back tears and whispering in her ear, "I don't know what to say to you." She said, "You don't have to say anything. All you have to do is be here."

CHARLIE: Lorrie is a strong woman and always has been. This had really gotten to her though. She seemed very vulnerable. Her barrier wasn't up. Yet she was still composed that day. She gave us each a big hug and said, "I love you guys. You have always been so nice to the both of us." Our hearts were breaking when she led us inside to view the body. People so often say this, but Keith honestly looked like he was asleep. It seemed so senseless: so much talent, and a guy Lorrie loved so much. Now he was lying dead in his casket. The three of us stood there for a length of time I can't measure, and then Lorianne and I left.

Looking back, I guess we had inklings that things were not going well for him. It was well known in the industry that Keith had been in this drinking culture since he was a teenager. Alcoholism had run in his family. Lorrie has told us since then that she and his doctors were convinced that he had a chemical addiction. There are some people who can take a drink or two and stop, and some whose body chemistry makes them crave more. Some, like Keith, apparently crave lethal dosages of it. We knew he had been battling the problem. But all the while we knew him, he seemed to be a happy, carefree guy. We always had the best time with him. We never saw him drunk. We never even saw him tipsy.

I remember hearing the rumors that he was drinking again. He seemed to run hot and cold. We'd hear that he would get passed-out, crazy drunk. His drinking would drive Lorrie to the brink.

LORIANNE: I recall an incident that occurred the last time Lorrie was on our show before his death. It was maybe a month or so before he died. I was walking past her dressing room. Her door was open and I could overhear her conversation; she must have been talking to her publicist or manager. I heard her say, "What do I do if Charlie or Lorianne ask me where Keith is?" Then I vaguely heard Lorrie say, "Well, I guess I'll tell them he's out . . . he's way out." I knew by the tone of her voice that something was very wrong.

I told Charlie what I overheard and we decided not to ask about Keith. I never told Lorrie that I had heard her, but I'm glad I did. Normally, we would have asked her about Keith. We would typically ask questions like "What are the two of you doing? Are you planning to have any more babies?" But we avoided the subject of her home life that night.

About a month or two after his death, Lorrie had me over to her house for one of the hardest interviews I have ever done. It's difficult to talk about it even now, after all this time. Lorrie started the interview by telling me about the moment she first heard of Keith's death.

She was touring somewhere up north when she got the call, from their manager, Jack McFadden. She had been feeling strangely all day, and she said she knew instinctively that the news was grim. Keith had not been doing well. He had been on a lot of binges. It had gotten so bad that when they went to bed at night, she would tie a sheet to his foot and tie the other end to her foot so she would know if he got up in the middle of the night. He would sometimes sneak out of bed, locate some of his stash, turn it up and down it.

While she was home, she did everything she could to keep him away from the bottle. She was fearful of what would happen when she left on tour but she had to work. She had commitments. She said, "My road manager came and told me that Jack was on the phone for me. I picked up the receiver and said, "Keith is dead, isn't he?"

Lorrie knew. She knew where he was headed. She told me that when she left to do that particular concert, she had a horrible feeling inside. She knew he was on a downhill slide. She said she will feel guilty the rest of her life for leaving on that trip. On the other hand, she knew that at some point he had to be on his own. She knew she couldn't follow him around and keep tying a bed sheet to their legs to save him. At some point, he had to save himself.

CHARLIE: Maybe he thought he didn't think he needed help. That's what happens with a lot of alcoholics. He had reportedly gone maybe two months without drinking and probably thought "I've got a handle on this." The next thought is "Maybe if I drink for just this one time it won't hurt."

LORIANNE: The problem is that a chemically addicted person can drink enough in one day to kill himself. That's what happened to Keith. After Lorrie and I talked about this whole thing for about an hour, we sat and just sobbed.

She was pretty strong until she talked about how Keith's death had impacted the kids. Their daughter, Morgan, was eight and old enough to understand what had happened. Lorrie talked about the times when she was driving Morgan to school, or they were going to get a burger, and she'd notice her crying. When she asked what was wrong, Morgan would say, "I miss Daddy." Lorrie had her hands full. She had to help her kids get through the worst times, and she had to get herself through it. She also had to keep her career going.

She said, "It's hard enough for me as a wife to deal with it, but how do I deal with little Jesse Keith?" She told me she and Keith had worked hard to create that baby. She had tried for a long time to get pregnant. She said the hardest times for her were when the baby asked about his daddy. He knew Keith usually got home from the road on Monday or Tuesday. So every Monday and Tuesday, little Jesse would look at her and ask, "Daddy come home today? Daddy come home?" She said that the questions would just wreck her. Each time she tried to explain, "No, Jesse, Daddy's not coming home. Daddy's in heaven." Of course, Jesse had no concept of what she was trying to say and he would beg her to see Daddy and kiss Daddy. Lorrie let him kiss Keith's picture. It was a heartbreaking scene that she had to play every week.

Something else that nearly put her over the edge was an incident that occurred after she got home from burying Keith. When I was at the Whitley home, she took me into the bedroom where he had died. She told me this story, standing in that room: "After I got back to the house, there was a knock at the door. It was the ambulance attendants. They had brought back the bed sheets they had used to carried Keith out. They were the sheets he had vomited on. Lorianne, you are not going to believe this, but the sheets still had his vomit on them. They didn't even clean them up before they brought them back to me." When they had handed her Keith's sheets, she said, she nearly lost it.

Frankly, I was surprised that Lorrie would do such a detailed interview so soon after Keith's death. But she truly believed that he had a chemical addiction, and that his story might help others get professional help.

None of this is meant to be morbid, or to exploit anyone's grief. It illustrates how people in our industry grieve together and pull together. There isn't a soul that's not touched when we lose one of our friends. You can feel the dark mood settling over the whole town. Dottie West, whose voice and openness endeared her to so many, died from injuries received in a car accident, a fluke of timing and trust.

CHARLIE: We had a tough time determining how to report Dottie's death. The accident happened late at night after our show and we learned about it like everyone else, from listening to the news. Dottie was on her way to the Opry. As I understand it, her car broke down and a gentleman visiting Nashville stopped and offered her a ride. It wasn't unusual for her to do something like that. She was a short distance from the Opry, so she probably figured, "Why not take the ride?"

From what we heard, he didn't make the curve when they took the exit to come to the park. When I first heard about the crash, it didn't seem all that serious. It was reported that she was injured, but there was no mention of her being critical. Then, as the days went by, her condition seemed to get worse on a daily basis.

LORIANNE: I remember a press conference when one of Dottie's doctors said, "It doesn't look good. We can't stop the bleeding." At that point, she had come out of surgery and the doctors had done as much as they could to patch her up. I think her spleen was damaged.

She was conscious when they took her into surgery the second time, and supposedly the doctors told her they needed her help. She needed to keep fighting. She needed to think about getting stronger. The doctors were hoping to get Dottie's mind-body connection going because *they* couldn't stop the bleeding. That was the last time she was conscious.

The doctors held several press conferences to report on her condition. At one briefing, a doctor said that Dottie was not doing well and that she might not make it.

That was a stunning announcement, so naturally we reported it. We didn't think about the impact this news might have on her family until after Dottie had died and we were at the funeral home. As it turned out, the information was accurate. Dottie died after that second attempt to stop the bleeding. But our accuracy didn't make the report any less painful for her daughter, Shelly.

CHARLIE: Lorianne and I went to the funeral home together. We have relationships with artists that really don't include our spouses. So in these situations, we go together because our presence represents not only our friendship but our business.

LORIANNE: All of Dottie's family was there. We went to her casket and paid our respects, then went back to see Shelly and her husband, Garry Hood. They were sitting in a separate room. When Shelly saw us, she came over and we all put our arms around each other like a football huddle. Shelly was speaking in a voice so faint it was barely a whisper. I could tell she was on another plane emotionally. She may have been in shock. What she said next nearly stopped my heart. She told us she had been watching our news reports on Dottie. She saw us report that Dottie would probably die and it had dashed all her hopes for her mother's recovery. She asked Charlie and me, "What did the doctors know about her? How dare they come out and say that she wasn't going to make it?"

I know Shelly wasn't angry at the doctors or at us. She was angry at losing her mother. But I could hear the hurt in her voice. When Charlie and I left the room, I felt so badly that I started crying in the hallway. I pictured her in front of the TV listening to our stinging words, "Dottie probably won't survive."

CHARLIE: I saw how upset Lorianne was over this and I took her over to a corner to talk. I tried to reassure her that what we had done was simply report what had been given to us. I told her that we had a responsibility to provide the facts to our viewers. I told her that it was possible that somehow Shelly may not have gotten the information regarding her mother's condition before the press conference. If Shelly found out from watching our show, it shouldn't have been that way, she should have been getting correct information from the doctors and hospital. Shelly hoped and expected her mother was going to pull through. Or maybe she had tuned out the reality of what was happening. It's human nature to do that. I don't think she meant what she said in an accusing way.

LORIANNE: At the time I did that report, I was focused on presenting the facts. It didn't cross my mind that Shelly might be watching. The reason I got so upset at the funeral home was because it hit me, for the first time, that I hurt her by the way we reported the story. Maybe I could have worded it less harshly.

CHARLIE: But you didn't hurt Shelly. The facts hurt her. In tragic situations like this one, the families are being protected by their management, by the Grand Ole Opry personnel, by nearly everybody. We can't know what they know. We only make assumptions. We can't call and ask her what she knows. That is not the time to be bothering the family members.

This kind of crisis is an example of the fine line we have to walk.

Sometimes reality is harsh, but we still have to report on it. What we do for a living affects well-known people who also happen to be our friends. We know their families. But we have to do our job.

LORIANNE: That incident was a turning point for me. I'm glad Shelly said something. I realize that we have to be aware of how we report sensitive events. We have to do more than just report the facts. We should include some compassion.

CHARLIE: We also got some letters complaining about the obituary that we did on Dottie after she died. In our report, we traced her life story, the good and the bad. We used footage of Dottie standing on the courthouse steps when her home was auctioned off. For the record, Dottie had personally called us and asked that our cameras be there. The footage showed Dottie in tears as a result of her financial troubles. A couple of irate fans sent letters saying "My God, the woman is dead. Why are you rehashing her troubles and dragging her through the mud?"

But I disagreed with those observations. We didn't drag her through the mud. Because we were doing a tribute, we had an obligation to tell the audience the details of her life story—both good and bad.

LORIANNE: One of the last interviews she did was on *Crook and Chase,* after she had gone through her financial trials. If we hadn't known what she had been through, we would never have guessed that she had a care in the world based on her appearance that night. In her usual fashion, she was all decked out in a fur hat and a jacket with fur around the collar. She was spectacular looking.

I remember her sitting there, saying that it didn't matter what the IRS had done to her. She said, "I always have a home when I walk out on that stage." She was talking about the relationship with her fans. I thought that was such a brave attitude to have. She wasn't teary-eyed and she wasn't asking for pity. She had a look of strength. She said, no matter what happened in her private life, it couldn't keep her off the stage. That was a very telling statement about her philosophy of life.

CHARLIE: She was country music's glamour lady. She brought a lot of attention to this industry with her bold steps, and country music isn't the same without her.

LORIANNE: Country music isn't the same without Roger Miller either. He was a mega-star. To be in his presence was thrilling because his mind was so quick. We had been informed of his surgery for throat cancer, but before anyone realized how serious it was, he was dead.

CHARLIE: There wasn't anything he couldn't do. He was one of those talents so big that wherever he was, on or off the stage, his presence filled the room. If Roger Miller walked in a door behind me, I would probably know he was here without turning around. His personality was larger than life.

LORIANNE: If anybody ever had the right to have an ego, it was Roger Miller. But he didn't. He took the time to make other people feel special. The first time we met him, he came up to us and said, "You kids are the best. You're very funny. I watch your show all the time." He would say those things on the air, and he would proceed to have a fabulous time with us on the set. He was the same way backstage. There wasn't a bigger compliment than one that came from Roger Miller.

CHARLIE: He was confident that he could do whatever he wanted. Here's a man who wrote some of the most original songs in the world, like "Chug a-lug" and classics like "King of the Road," and then turned around and wrote a Broadway musical. He knew that he had a talent that could be applied to different formats.

He chose to make music with his God-given talent. Country was his musical home. But he had crossover pop success with songs like "England Swings." He was smart enough to realize that the simplicity of his songs was closer to the country music style. He wrote the Broadway play, *Big River,* and the lyrics, the presentation, and the music, all had a country flair to it. The country sound was always present in his music, and he knew how to decorate it.

LORIANNE: It's hard to believe that at one time, Roger, along with Waylon Jennings, Willie Nelson, and Kris Kristofferson were practically starving. (And could anyone name a more interesting group of starving artists?) They packed what little they had along with their instruments and traveled around the country trying to get whatever gig they could. Each of them became famous in his own way. But during those lean times, they propped each other up. They celebrated the good times and lamented the bad times together. They developed an intricate bonding that tied Roger to the whole country music industry.

CHARLIE: Country was where his friends were. I have a suspicion that Roger was the kind of guy who would rather have had a good friend than a big-hit song any day of the week.

LORIANNE: This story will give you an insight into Roger Miller. We taped the *Crook and Chase* show every afternoon at 2:30 in front of a live audience, and then it aired at 6:30 that night. Once, when Roger was scheduled to be our guest, it snowed. Six to eight inches of snow had fallen and the streets froze over. But the show must go on. Our limo picked Roger up at the Vanderbilt Plaza and brought him over to the studio. Our audience seated over one hundred people. *Two* showed up that day! We asked the limo driver to sit in the audience just to fill up another seat.

CHARLIE: After we added a couple of staff members there were maybe five people in the audience. Roger turned what could have been an embarrassing situation into something that was fun. We had a wonderful time, laughing and giggling. We explained to the viewers about how the bad weather had kept most of our audience at home, then we introduced Roger. As Roger Miller, mega-star, walked out, five people were clapping. Roger thought it was hilarious.

LORIANNE: A lesser person than Roger may have canceled, feeling it wasn't worth the time. But he took it by the tail and ran with it, joking about his limo driver in the audience. It was one of the funniest shows we ever did. Roger was the best.

CHARLIE: I think Roger may have spent most of his life bored. He was so creative, he spent a lot of his life searching for something. He found fulfillment toward the end of his life. One of the last times he came on our show, he brought his wife, Mary, and a picture of their baby. He was a proud papa late in life. That baby was all he talked about.

LORIANNE: It was amazing to see the transformation in him. I had heard the stories about his heavy drug phase; he told me most of them himself. But I knew him as the guy who was devoted to his wife and baby.

One time he came on our show wearing a big watch that featured his baby daughter's face. He showed it to the cameras. Then he grabbed the guitar and sang some of the nonsensical, lullaby-type songs that he had made up to please and thrill his little daughter.

CHARLIE: There was a lot of do-dooby-do, do-dooby-do. He had professional success in his back pocket. He had achieved everything else and during those last few years he was looking for the personal success. He had found that. I think he had found everything he was looking for before he died.

LORIANNE: Roger was fulfilling a lot of things later in life because during his earlier years he had gotten involved with drugs and alcohol. Substance abuse messed him up so badly that he had a four- or five-year dry spell when he couldn't write anything. He told me that period had been terribly painful for him. I tried to broach the topic in an interview one time to find out what that period of his life was like, and he looked at me and said, "I don't think I want to explain all that." I got the impression that it still hurt him to think that he had wasted so much time. He wanted to get on with his life and fulfill himself with his wife and the baby and his friends.

CHARLIE: But Roger could joke about that period of his life. There was one Rogerism that I remember in particular. He would say, "Never keep your pills and your loose change in the same pocket because I just swallowed thirty-five cents." He lived some wild days back in the 1960s.

LORIANNE: Roger would talk about those wild days. He would tell a Kris Kristofferson, Roger, and Willie Nelson story at the drop of a hat. There was a time when he, Kris, and Willie were drinking in a hotel room. They were being so loud that the management had called and told them they were going to have to settle down because they were bothering people on the rest of the floor. Well, they didn't settle down. So finally there was a loud knock on the door. They all knew it had to be the police.

Roger then told how Willie, who he said was drunk or stoned or both, stumbled to the door and grabbed the knob and yanked the door open. Sure enough, it was the police. Roger recalled that Willie immediately sobered up. The policeman said, "You've got to be quiet." Willie said,

"Yes, sir, yes, sir. We were writing songs here, sir. And we just didn't realize how loud we were. We'll be quiet, sir." Willie closed the door and immediately returned to his stupor. Willie had managed to act sober for about fifteen seconds, and then he fell apart. Roger said he laughed all night about that. He couldn't even tell the story without doubling over laughing. I truly wish Roger had written a book. But when I mentioned that to him, he said, "I can't write a book until everybody I know is dead because it would hurt so many people."

CHARLIE: We realized something was drastically wrong with Roger when we were backstage with him at the Academy of Country Music Awards in April 1992. He died later that year.

LORIANNE: We had heard about his throat surgery. We had been told that the growth was malignant, but the word had filtered back that he was fine. When we called his management company to ask about his condition, they said, "He has had the surgery and is recovering." They didn't lead us to believe anything else was wrong. But when we saw Roger backstage at the ACM Awards, he was withdrawn, not his usual exuberant self. His voice was hoarse, as if he had a sore throat. He spoke in a whisper: "Well, how are you? Great! I'll talk to you later." Then he walked away as fast as he could. I think he knew he was seriously ill and he didn't want us to see him that way. I turned to Charlie and said, "What's wrong?" His manner was so odd. He usually stood around and talked for an hour or so. But on that occasion, he turned away. Of course, we never saw him again. We've heard similar stories from other country stars. Roger didn't want anyone to know he was dying.

CHARLIE: Usually when we got together with Roger we were always laughing. There weren't ten seconds that went by without a quip. I'm sure on that night it was painful for him to have a normal conversation, more so to laugh. I think he was avoiding us for a lot of reasons but primarily because he was in pain.

LORIANNE: He may have known that was to be his last award show. I wish that he could have let us know he was in that kind of shape. Later, Waylon flew out to see Roger in the hospital and he told me it was such a shock. Medical personnel tried to prepare Waylon for how Roger would look: His face and head were distorted and swollen from the disease and the treatment. But Waylon said, "Nothing could have prepared me for his condition. I walked into the room and it was all I could do not to let my reaction show on my face. Though," he said, "in true Roger Miller fashion, once I sat down and started talking to him, Roger was making jokes about dying and trying to put me at ease."

There is no easy way to receive bad news and no good place to be when you get it. At times, a shock is dramatized by the minor and ordinary events of our daily lives.

CHARLIE: I will never forget how I heard that Conway Twitty had died. My son, Dave, and I had gone to a little general store near our home to pick up sausage and biscuits and a newspaper. I was driving my wife's car and the dial was set on an oldies radio station when I got in. It was playing Conway Twitty records.

The station was playing "Hello, Darlin'." After we got back from the grocery, I went into the house and heard a different radio station playing another Twitty record. Then I realized that the general store had been playing Conway's songs too, and I thought something must be up. I picked up the newspaper and it mentioned that Conway had been admitted to a hospital. After I had heard two more of his songs on the radio, I thought "Oh no, he's dead."

I immediately flipped the dial to WSM. I knew the station that carried the Grand Ole Opry would be doing a tribute if anything had happened. That was when I first found out he had died.

I was startled by the cause of his death. Nobody knew there had been anything wrong with him. He died of an intestinal aneurysm. When I heard that, I thought "Darn, how do you die from that?" But as I understand it, when an artery explodes, a person's chances of survival are nil. I called Jim and said, "Have you heard about Conway?" He said, "Yeah, I read in the paper this morning that he's in the hospital." I said, "No, he's dead."

LORIANNE: It was a weekend when we found out that Conway had died.

When Jim heard about Conway, he woke me up to tell me. I called one of our other producers, Ray Sells, to confirm what had happened. I asked, "Is it true?" My blood ran cold as he answered, "I'm afraid he's dead."

Once I heard that, we all went into action. I was the executive producer of *Crook and Chase* and I knew that we had to start putting together an hour-long tribute show for airing on Monday night. All of our wonderful producers and writers raced into the office. I didn't even take a shower that morning. I put a hat on over my greasy hair and headed for work. I stopped to pick up bananas and orange juice. Somebody else brought doughnuts and bagels. Everybody came in. We weren't crying, but we were somber.

We scrapped everything that had been planned for the Monday night show and created an entire hour-long tribute to Conway Twitty. We went into our vault to pull video footage. We all had a strong sense of purpose that day.

Producing a tribute show is very strange and touchy. Our staff has had to do this on several occasions. There is a lot of pressure because it has to be pulled together quickly. People are running around like crazy, making phone calls, typing and editing. I remember sitting in my office thinking, while I was typing, a lot of people go to the funeral or they stand by the coffin to pay their respects. But sitting there, seeing the whole show come together, made me think, "This is the best way that we can show our respect and admiration for Conway . . . to do our best to present his life and his career and his personality the way it really was."

It was so satisfying, the day after that show aired. Even Conway's family members, like his son, Michael Twitty, called in and said, "That was the best thing anybody did for Dad." To try to capture somebody's life and career, and to honor his memory for the rest of his fans, is a privilege.

CHARLIE: It is a tribute to our staff that they were able to produce such an excellent tribute at the last minute. In essence, we were doing four or five days of work, maybe more, crammed into one. A show like that requires a lot of extra preparation and thought. We were proud of the product that we took on the air with us that night.

If fate ever had a hand in the timing of a death, it had to have a hand in Conway Twitty's. He died the day before the first day of Fan Fair, probably his favorite time of the year because he was so fan-oriented. I heard so many people on Music Row say "My Lord, did he time this?" They said it as a loving tribute.

Lorianne and I were hosts for the celebrity softball game that Sunday afternoon, the day after he died. We announced that we would like to have a moment of silence for Conway Twitty. We did that and then said, "Conway loved the applause. So let's hear it for Conway Twitty one more time." The whole crowd of twenty-five thousand people got up and roared. I get chill bumps just thinking about it. That was really a memorable experience.

CHAPTER 11

And the Band Plays On

If Rand McNally tried to redraw the map of country music, the job would be unending. From our vantage point, here on the couch, we have seen the changes unfold, in the business and in the artists, and with them the cycles of success and failure.

We have reached a point where gold records are almost taken for granted. For many artists, the high jump bar has been raised to platinum. The pressure, the stakes, the money, all are magnified. Typically, it can cost a quarter of a million dollars or more to launch a career in country music today.

CHARLIE: The business is tougher than it used to be because there are more demands. I have seen artists literally stumbling from exhaustion, while getting off an airplane at seven in the morning. I have seen them get off those red-eye flights, arriving back in Nashville to squeeze in a few hours with the family before they take off again.

The aspiring artists need to do some research about what they are getting into. They certainly need to write their songs and hone their talent, but they also need to find out about the lifestyle. To survive today, an artist has to be strong emotionally, and smart. True, there are more conveniences today—traveling on airplanes instead of being cramped in the backseat of a car heading across country. But the business end is much more detailed. Hypothetically, I feel like most of them need to go to a Country Music Business College, and pass a written exam, before they cut their first record.

LORIANNE: It is so very different. I have heard George Jones talk about how the kids starting out today need to understand marketing, and the legal aspects of the business. He said artists today actually read their contracts, and understand what they are reading. George said when he was young, he just signed whatever was put in front of him. Of course, he and a lot of artists literally signed their lives away. Oftentimes, the managers and the record companies got the bulk of the money. The artists went on the road, worked themselves to the bone, and saw little of the profits.

CHARLIE: You know why? Because they were paid in cash back then. I've heard Bill Anderson's stories, how the promoters took the funds collected from ticket sales and gave cash to the artist's road manager. There was no way for anyone to know how much may have been skimmed off the top.

LORIANNE: There was no real accounting. The artists got what they got, and there was no record of how much money had been generated. Nowadays, they know exactly how much they have made. They can get rich almost overnight. Alan Jackson and Billy Ray Cyrus have invested wisely in real estate and in publishing and booking companies. They operate like businessmen. They haven't traded in their guitars for briefcases, but don't keep their cash in paper sacks, either.

CHARLIE: The key to a successful career these days is having a good manager. The reason I say that is because the artist has to have somebody direct the traffic that's headed toward him when he has a big hit. At that point, everybody wants a piece of the artist. So the artist needs somebody who has his best interest in mind, somebody who is a combination big brother and bodyguard. The manager needs to know when to say yes, and when to say no. They need X-ray vision, to be able to stand back and see how the future is going to be affected by what the artist is doing today.

What may come as a surprise to the public is that artists don't typically make that much money from record sales in relation to everything else. For the artist, the top-selling album is the catalyst for getting booked on the road. Touring the road is where the mother lode is. The manager needs to understand how to parlay a successful record into big bucks for the artist.

LORIANNE: Reba McEntire is a perfect example of how an artist has parlayed her hit records into a business that keeps growing. She will be the first to admit that she has come a long way, baby. Over the years, she has elevated her image to match the versatility of her voice, and that combination catapulted her into this superstar stratosphere where she is today.

CHARLIE: Country music outlets have broadened so much in recent years. It used to be that an artist could have one person who functioned as both the manager and the booking agent. That's all that was needed. There were few opportunities for television appearances. The artists didn't have Hollywood begging them to do movies, as what happened with the *Maverick* movie. Sure, you had Roy Acuff doing the B pictures, but nothing on the scope of what is being done now. So one person could handle all the demands and he probably snapped up any opportunity that came along because they were so few and far between. Country artists didn't get the endorsements that they are offered today. Now, all offers have to be analyzed because a better one might come in tomorrow.

LORIANNE: Many artists today have their own stylist who picks out their clothes, hairstyle, and makeup. When you see what looks like a star's entourage, you are seeing a professional support group that has a big impact on the star's image and career.

CHARLIE: An artist's looks are going to change as his or her career changes. Lorrie Morgan is a perfect example. She got her break because of her talent. Then she started changing her looks. She has gone from looking like a pretty down-home country girl to a glamorous woman. It is the artists' music that first draws attention. Then the artists can make an easier transition, if they desire, to whatever they think feels better for them.

LORIANNE: I have never seen a time when so much talent was out there. They all have a story. Tim McGraw is the son of a famous baseball pitcher, Tug McGraw, who helped the Phillies win the World Series. Tim can be a big star with staying power. He exudes confidence. He knows what makes his music work and he walks right out onstage and just does it.

When he was brand-new, Tim did an important TV show we hosted for high school students. We weren't prepared for the reaction he received. He strutted out there and had those kids clamoring for him, as they crowded the stage. He sang "Indian Outlaw" that night, and right away it set him apart because the sound was so different from anything else out there. Now he's a multimillion-selling artist. It's thrilling to watch a superstar unfold.

CHARLIE: Part of the reason for his confidence is the fact that he is seasoned. He knows what this business is all about. He had been singing "Indian Outlaw" for several years on the road, but he hadn't recorded it because he wasn't sure how it would be received. But he realized that the times had changed, and a really unusual song might have a chance to catch on. Tim knew what he was doing.

LORIANNE: Faith Hill is another example of somebody having the whole package. She is fresh-faced and excited by her newfound stardom, but she doesn't seem to be intimidated by the commotion going on around her.

CHARLIE: The first time she appeared on our show, she seemed real meek. Her hit, "Wild One," had just come out. She was pleasant, but cautious. I think she was still assessing the situation. The next thing I knew, she appeared on the *Letterman Show*. It wasn't long before she was making news with rumors about a romance with Troy Aikman. The rumors turned out to be untrue. Say this for Aikman: He's a private fellow, however some country singers would pay to get the news coverage he tries to avoid.

LORIANNE: We get asked about discovering new talent. We are flattered that many stars give us credit and personal thank-yous for helping to launch their careers. But the truth is, you don't "find" true talent. It finds you.

It isn't easy to predict where we see country music going during the next ten years. I've seen so many changes in the last ten years that no one anticipated. Think of how far the music has evolved when Faith Hill records an old Janis Joplin song, "Piece of My Heart." Artists today realize they can take any song, make it their own, and still have a sound that appeals to their audience.

CHARLIE: In the next decade, you might see country music have a lot of one-hit wonders, like pop music did in the 1960s. But there are also going to be artists who shine, who are going to stand out and stay in the limelight. We will see new stars emerging all the time, but out of the pack will emerge the new Reba McEntires and Randy Travises.

LORIANNE: The newer artists come from a much broader background than their predecessors. Vince Gill may record some songs that are very pop sounding, but he freely admits that he cut his teeth on bluegrass music and he loves standing on the Grand Ole Opry stage, performing alongside Jim and Jesse. John Michael Montgomery isn't afraid to admit that he grew up in the country, and poor, but he still listened to Led Zeppelin. So, every now and then, you're going to hear a Led Zeppelin guitar lick in one of his songs.

Country music stars today are real and they're honest. I think it is cool that the Kentucky Headhunters can say in the same breath that they love Bill Monroe *and* rock and roll music. So they take a Bill Monroe tune and make it rock. This mixture of musical influences is creating a unique kind of music. But the real reason I think it works is because these new artists are performing from the heart.

CHARLIE: The young stars have learned a lot from established stars like Brenda Lee, who grew up in the business, went through a rockabilly stage, and cabaret songs, and then returned to her roots. When you think about it, being around Brenda Lee is being around greatness. Here is a young lady who, at the age of eleven, was recording songs for Decca that were heard around the world. She toured with Elvis, and at one point the Beatles opened for Brenda Lee before they hit superstardom. So the lady is fun to talk to—she has so many things she can tell you about being a child star, and trying to have a normal teenage life, if there is such a thing for a top recording artist.

LORIANNE: She's proof it never has to be over. So is John Anderson. Here is a guy who had success several years ago with the songs "Swingin'" and "Old Chunk of Coal." Then his career took a nosedive.

CHARLIE: In this business, an artist can go from zipping along at one hundred miles an hour to sitting on zero, real quick. John seemed to vanish from the scene for maybe a decade. Everybody thought he had quit. But we found out in an interview with him that during those years he was always out performing somewhere. He didn't lose his edge. Sometimes, if an artist gets away from performing he has difficulty coming back. Now, John wasn't playing the major arenas. He was playing little honky-tonks, but he kept himself employed. He kept his band employed. Then, all of a sudden, he had the song, "Straight Tequila Night," that brought him back.

LORIANNE: He left open the possibility of coming back because he wasn't bitter. He didn't go into a corner and curse the industry. When he was out of the limelight, he stayed home a lot. He said that he got back his religion that he had left behind. He worked on creating a stronger foundation with his wife and children. So he spent his time wisely. I really believe the things that he did were part of a building process. He was rebuilding his character, which in turn contributed to his musical skills. That process has a kind of domino effect. He realized that the reason he wasn't on top anymore wasn't because of the industry, or the record label, or his manager. So he went to work on the one area he could control, and change—himself.

CHARLIE: He was trying to survive and he wanted to stay involved in the music that he dearly loved. It may have been unconscious on his part, but it kept him strong, and now he is back to where he was, even bigger than before.

LORIANNE: You hear the old phrase "You've got to pay your dues." Well, each star finds he or she has to ante up in his or her own way.

CHARLIE: Ray Price was controversial back in the sixties. They said he was pushing the envelope of country music with too much orchestration. Turns out he was on target. I also view Ray as part of country music's early rat pack, when you think about it.

Willie Nelson on guitar and Buddy Emmons on the steel guitar were at one time a part of Ray's band, the Cherokee Cowboys, which turned out so many great artists. He was kind of like the Dean Martin or Frank Sinatra of country music, in that he gave a lot of guys their start. He ascended to the top and stayed there. The hits just rolled out—among them the classic "For the Good Times," written by a then unknown named Kris Kristofferson. Everybody wanted to be in the same league as Ray Price. As the saying goes, no one is sure what league that is, but it doesn't take long to call the roll.

LORIANNE: Ray Price obviously had a large vision for country. In many ways it has come to pass.

Charlie and I were asked to host the Golden Apple Awards in Hollywood—a pretty big deal for us. Charlton Heston, Tom Cruise, Geana Davis, and Bridget Fonda were on the show. We were asked to bring along a country music artist who would do an acoustic performance. The first person we thought of was Gary Morris because he has such a great voice, and because of his ties to Hollywood, and series TV.

After we introduced Gary, he walked up to the podium and said, "I'm sure this audience is aware of the movie *Beaches*. Bette Midler had a hit with the film's theme song, 'Wind Beneath My Wings.' While a lot of you think that she was the first to have a hit with that song, actually I had the country hit with it first. I thought you'd like to hear how that song should really go."

What he said was tongue in cheek. Everybody there laughed, and were knocked out by his performance. I consider him a fabulous singer and songwriter. And I have a memory of him that I think says so much about the business, and the importance of having your work accepted.

I was flying back from doing a video shoot with Clint Black, in Texas.

It was about six o'clock in the morning, way too early. When I boarded my connecting flight to Nashville, I saw Gary. There was hardly anybody else on the plane other than me, my crew, and Gary. After a little bit, Gary came over and sat next to me. He had a Walkman with a tape of his new album. He said, "This is a rough cut, but I want your opinion."

So I put on the headphones and started listening. Once I hit the play button, I was aware that Gary was right in my face, watching my expression. The harder he stared, the more embarrassed and uncomfortable I began to feel. I listened to a couple of songs and said, "These are beautiful!"

Very seriously, with a hint of disappointment, he said, "But there was no expression on your face."

He was bothered that I wasn't showing any emotion. I felt a little guilty, but frankly it's hard for me to show emotion before breakfast, with someone staring at me from four inches away. Finally, I turned away from him and looked out the window. I don't remember the exact songs, but I lost myself in his voice, listening as the plane ascended through the clouds. It was a gorgeous day, sunny with a very blue sky. His voice seemed to soar with the plane. It was a very moving moment, but I guess it just didn't come through on my face.

CHARLIE: One of my favorites is Tom T. Hall. He had written "Harper Valley PTA" for Jeannie C. Riley and, as I never get tired of recalling, she was the first artist I ever interviewed. So we had a connection.

Tom and his wife, Miss Dixie, have a place called Fox Hollow, not far from either Lorianne or myself. We're kind of neighbors, and we see him around town in his Jeep, with his boots and hat and a plug of tobacco. He performs only when he wants to these days. He loves to farm and play golf and every now and then I join him for eighteen holes. One day, I couldn't help but think "Here's a guy who wrote one of the most popular songs probably in the history of music, and here I am, playing golf with him, trying to stay out of the sand trap."

Tom T. is called the "Storyteller," because he can write songs or books. I so admire someone with the ability to tell a story. Think of it: he wrote a three-minute song, "Harper Valley PTA," and he put enough in there to make a two-hour television movie out of it. His is one of the most brilliant minds in music. I liken him to Roger Miller.

LORIANNE: There is an interesting blend in country music of the macho side and the sentimental side. One of the most touching moments I have ever seen was the night that Alan Jackson accepted the Song of the Year award on the Music City News Country Songwriters Award Show. He had won for the song "I'd Love You All Over Again," which he wrote for his wife, Denise. It was their tenth wedding anniversary. Denise was sitting in the front row and she had just recently had their first baby, Mattie. Since the song won, Alan sang it. And when he was singing, his voice started quivering.

After the awards were over, Charlie and I interviewed him and we asked about his performance. We could tell that he was embarrassed. No performer likes to let his emotions get the best of him. He told us that while he was singing he saw Denise in the front row and he started to choke up. He was afraid he wouldn't get through the song. He kept singing through his emotion and felt that it was not one of his best performances. The fans saw it differently. They felt it was one of his best because it so obviously and poignantly came straight from the heart.

CHARLIE: It was an example of how genuine these people are. Some performances are contrived. But that was definitely not the case with Alan Jackson that night.

LORIANNE: That performance was what country music is all about. Alan had no reason to be ashamed of showing his heart. After our interview, Alan was hanging around and he said, "Denise married me when she was seventeen years old. I dragged her away from her family to live in a basement for five years. No one can know what she means to me, or what she has been through, but she stuck with me." I think he was truly amazed that this woman loved him enough to leave a comfortable home with her parents to live in a basement with an unemployed singer and songwriter.

CHARLIE: Another point that needs to be made is that country music fans are fairly forgiving. Johnny Paycheck was truly thrilled at having a second chance at his career, after that tragic barroom scrape, which ended with Johnny shooting a guy and going to prison. He was a model prisoner and the first appearance he made out of prison was a night I was subbing for Ralph on *Nashville Now*. George Jones was on as well, basically to support Johnny, who was knee-shaking scared. He didn't know how the public was going to react; didn't know how he was going to sound.

When Paycheck came on, he performed "Take This Job and Shove It," his trademark song, and then he came over and sat down during the commercial break. He was breathing like he had just run a marathon. On the air he admitted he was nervous, and, by admitting all the apprehension he had, I think the fans quickly accepted him back. They didn't approve what he did, of course, and he served time for it. But he was willing to come back and try to get his career started again; he was clean, wasn't doing drugs, alcohol, anything. I think they admired that and they gave him the second chance he wanted. So he's still out doing some work, making some appearances and some movies.

Nashville is a town where strong men are not afraid to cry. It's a town with a lot of "meat 'n threes"—places where they serve a meat and three vegetables at a reasonable price. You can drop in for lunch and run into a member of the Country Music Hall of Fame. And more than likely he will invite you to sit down with him.

CHARLIE: Once, we were in a meat-'n-three, my wife, Karen, and my kids, Rachael and David, sitting at the table next to Eddy Arnold. He wanted to meet my family, which prompted him to come sit down at our table. Rachael was then six or seven years old, and he started singing an old song from the forties I had never heard before, "Rachel, Rachel, I've been thinking . . ." He went on and on, and Rachael was just tickled to death. She sat there mesmerized. She was too young to appreciate that here was one of the top recording artists in the world, of all time, serenading her. One of these days, she will look back and see the real magic and joy in that moment.

LORIANNE: My most vivid memory of Eddy Arnold is actually a scene from television. Years ago, before I knew Eddy as well as we know him now, I saw him on an awards show. They were honoring him for his lifetime achievements in music. He must have known that he was being honored that night, yet when he walked to the stage from the audience something happened that I will never forget.

As the entire audience rose and cheered in unison, Eddy broke down and started crying before he even reached the podium. He stood there in tears before this wildly enthusiastic ovation. It lasted two minutes or more, which is an eternity in television.

When he finally opened his mouth to speak, in a quivering voice, he said, "I'm a sentimental man." Then he broke down again. It was such a real and tender moment, a man touched by the fans and industry that *he* had touched for so many years.

That incident tells you a lot about the kind of man Eddy Arnold is. He pulls no punches. He never masks his feelings, good or bad, and you can always count on him to shoot straight with you. In fact, I once called his office because I wanted to do an interview with him. It was his voice on the answering machine that told me to leave a message when I heard "the little beep." Eddy himself called back the next day to say yes, he would do an interview with me, but no, he couldn't do it right away. I didn't have to go 'round and 'round with layers of managers and publicists. Eddie knows what he wants to be involved in and what he doesn't and he will tell you up front. I appreciate that approach. Most of us do. It saves everyone a lot of time and energy.

I don't mean to sound star-struck. But when you realize all he has accomplished—with record sales in the same league as Elvis and the Beatles—and never lost his sweetness, you know this is someone in a league of his own.

He makes no bones about the fact that he came from a dirt-poor background, which may explain why he is so shrewd when it comes to money. It is common knowledge in the music industry that Eddy invested well, especially in real estate, and managed his investments wisely. However, he doesn't talk much about finances. I respect him for the fact that he doesn't flaunt his personal business, with one exception. He loves to talk about his yacht. He and his wife, Sally, spend a lot of time traveling the waterways and it seems a grand source of peacefulness for both of them.

His most consistent piece of advice to people in show business is never to lend money, on the theory that lending money is one of the leading causes of amnesia.

CHARLIE: A magic moment for both of us was the day we went to see Minnie Pearl at her home. She had suffered a massive stroke, as everybody knows. It affected one side of her body, but she is still mentally alert. We called over to see how she was doing and ended up talking to Henry, her husband. He got on the phone and said, "Why don't you guys come over and see Miss Minnie?" So we did.

LORIANNE: When we arrived, Minnie was in bed next to the window. She was watching the birds. She has a bird feeder in front of a wide-open window. Her room is painted a soft yellow. Her bedspread is yellow. I was impressed with how pretty her hair was. And she had on bright red lipstick. The first thing she sees when she opens her eyes in the morning is a beautiful portrait of herself with Henry, hanging on the wall in front of her.

CHARLIE: She has autographed pictures everywhere, including a photo of Burt Reynolds on the wall. It just so happens that we visited her the same day that Earl Scruggs and his wife were there. We got to hear all of these stories about the old days, of them traveling around and the shows they did together. Henry, Minnie's husband, had been a pilot, so they were talking about how Henry would fly them into these small airstrips, where they had to circle around a mountain and then drop down almost immediately in order to hit the runway. They told some really funny stories. Miss Minnie was having a good ole time, sitting there in her bed, just laughing. I went over and held her hand and she would squeeze it because I've always been one of the "fellers." Miss Minnie has always joked about chasing men, and I always brag that I never did run too fast. Miss Minnie is the epitome of a southern belle. This is a remarkable woman, a class act.

In our twelve years as a team, we have done around four thousand interviews—obviously, several with the same stars. We appreciate them all. They provide us with an unending flow of music and news. We try to repay them with fairness and a friendly place to chat.

Of course, not all of the guests we, and our fans, have enjoyed are involved in country music. Here are some memories of a couple of our favorites.

KIRK DOUGLAS: Kirk came on our show to talk about his book, a novel called *The Gift*. After our interview, he told us this was the first time during his promotional tour that he actually got to talk about his book. Other interviewers had concentrated on his movie career. We talked a bit about movies but emphasized the book. Besides, he's a wonderful storyteller, and after reading the book you could picture Kirk Douglas and his son Michael doing a movie version of the story. It has always been talked about. If they could put a script together, the two of them would be wonderful together. If you look at pictures of Kirk Douglas when he was the same age as Michael is now, they look just alike. It is a really fascinating family.

MINNESOTA FATS: Rudolf Wanderone (his real name) moved to Nashville back in the eighties. He was one of those mainstays, who always liked to be seen around the country music stars. He doesn't sign autographs. He has one of those ink pads, with a stamp that has his signature written on it. This is partly out of convenience, and partly because his capacity to write his name has declined over the years. You ask for an autograph and he will whip out his ink pad, ask for a piece of paper, and stamp his name on it.

Charlie played against him in a match one time on Channel 4 when he first came to town. He let Charlie run three or four balls in the hole, then after he missed, Fats ran the table and beat him. Even in his declining age and health, the Fat Man is still brash and cocky. He talks about being the greatest pool player who ever walked the face of the earth and not many will argue with him.

He always carries his memories in his inside coat pocket—a lot of newspaper and magazine articles that have been laminated, all the legendary stories that have appeared about Fats and Willie Mosconi and all the other greats. He is quite a character. You start talking about the past and he will unload his pockets and give you a show there for about thirty minutes.

Of all our guests, if we had to pick the one who came out of a different box, who has the most unusual and offbeat talent, the winner would be Tiny Tim.

CHARLIE: Again, I was subbing for Ralph when I first met Tiny Tim. I introduced him and he trilled and strummed and charmed the audience with his one hit, "Tiptoe Through the Tulips." Then, all during the interview he referred to me as "Mr. Chase, oh, Mr. Chase." He brought me tulips, his gesture of kindness. The thing about Tiny Tim that amazes people is his age. It's hard to get a readout on this man because of his image and his look. He doesn't appear that old. He turned seventy-three in early April 1995, which meant he was in his sixties when he did *Nashville Now* with me. And he talked about drinking olive oil every day to help keep his skin young-looking. There might be something to that. But he was quite an unusual personality, to put it mildly.

LORIANNE: When Tiny Tim was a guest on *Crook and Chase*, I was taken by what a sweet man he is. I instantly understood why he was a frequent guest on Johnny Carson's show. Tiny seems to be a very sincere person, all wrapped up in a rather unusual package. He was exactly the same backstage as he was when the cameras rolled. He was very polite to me, always calling me Miss Lorianne.

I must admit, though, that before we actually met in the studio makeup room I was worried about whether or not I would be able to relate to him, and carry on a conversation with him. After all, he has that dyed red hair, he wears more makeup than I do, and dresses in what looks to me like a zoot suit from the fifties. But the minute he offered me his hand and said, "Very pleased to meet you, Miss Lorianne," I knew that I was dealing with a very real person.

Although Tiny is obviously unlike the average Joe, to me he doesn't seem aware of the differences. When he sings in that falsetto voice, and plays his ukelele, people usually laugh. Tiny seems to be clearly pleased to be entertaining the audience. I like him because he seems to be comfortable in his own skin.

You have to wonder how a guy who is so noticeable goes about doing the mundane tasks of life—going to the bank, filling up the gas tank, picking up groceries. In the interview, he said he just does what he needs to do, and if people stare he will smile and talk to them, but other than that he just goes on about his life. Tiny Tim strikes me as childlike in many ways, and I mean that as a compliment—he's a sweet and innocent being. One of my favorite gifts is an autographed ukelele he gave me after the interview.

These are but a few of the remarkable people we have the good fortune to work with every day. It's no wonder we both feel the same way . . . we can't wait to get to work tomorrow.

Epilogue

As we put the finishing touches on this book, we find ourselves surrounded by controversy and rumors. By now you have read somewhere that we have decided to end our long relationship with TNN, The Nashville Network. Our run lasted ten years, covering three shows, and they were happy and successful years, almost to the day that we announced we were not coming back to TNN. We would not renew our contract.

The date was May 9, 1995, and our producer, Jim Owens, gave as the reason for our decision "creative and philosophical" differences.

When people in show business hear the phrase "creative differences," usually one word pops into their heads: money.

But this disagreement was not about money—we really didn't get that far. It was, in fact, about creative differences—how the show looked, how we looked. It was about style and image, not substance. There really were no villains. A new management took over at TNN just after we had gone on the air with *Music City Tonight,* the network's flagship show. The new management team wanted to make changes with which we disagreed. That happens.

It is seldom easy to leave a place where you feel you have been successful, where you have set goals and exceeded them, and developed a bond with the staff and the crews and, most of all, the fans. We have been love-bombed by the letters that poured in. The fans in country music are the best. They can't really understand why we are leaving, but they are upset and they support us.

There is no need to get into a point-by-point recital of all the issues. They are important only to the people who were being asked to deal with them. But we owe it to our audience, and to the artists who appeared on the show, to make it clear that the decision was ours and we didn't make it lightly.

In brief, the differences appeared before the negotiations to renew our contract were seriously under way. Two weeks before Christmas, in 1994, the network gave us an ultimatum to fire the brass section from our band. In their opinion, horns are not country. We fought that directive, lost, then argued to delay the order until after Christmas. We lost again.

In matters that are meant to be strictly business, you remind yourself not to take things personally. But the network wanted us, as hosts, to change our image. They sent us pictures clipped from magazines and clothing samples to show us how we should look. They wanted us in Western wear by April 1, 1995. This we could not do. Our image is us. We haven't dressed "country" in all the years we've been on television. We didn't wear jeans or fringe or boots because it simply wasn't us. It's a great look for millions of people who are expressing their personal style, whether it be for work or a night out at a dance club. But we express our own style, and we've been successful in spreading the message that you don't have to play-act by dressing country in order to understand and love country music. Anybody will tell you that, first and foremost, country music is built on honesty. We didn't want to look fake. We were the *hosts* of *Music City Tonight,* not one of the acts.

It almost sounds like a song—the clothes we wear, the way we comb our hair—but we found ourselves defending how we presented ourselves. Yet, *Music City Tonight* had improved a previously sluggish time slot and had seen the ratings make a dramatic increase. We also attracted more of what the network had prized—younger viewers.

Despite the success of the show, our entire staff faced what we all felt were serious problems behind the scenes. At TNN we broadcast, as did *Nashville Now*, out of a temporary facility that was basically a warehouse, with a roof that leaks on members of our studio audience. *Music City Tonight* tapes before six hundred studio guests every night, and many even had large structural poles blocking their view of the stage. The complaints came to us every night—continual, angry complaints that included uncomfortable bleacher seating and inadequate bathroom facilities. Even more frustrating were the many complaints from the stars themselves, their managers, and publicists. Suffice it to say that their backstage and dressing room areas leave much to be desired. It became difficult to try to do an upbeat, fun show when we were constantly having to apologize and make excuses to the stars and our audience. On numerous occasions, we informed Gaylord executives of these ongoing problems. Unfortunately, they still exist today and we are powerless to make our own improvements.

When we signed our original contract, we were informed that the Acuff Theater would be renovated and we would have a real theater to showcase our guests. That never happened. We were told that plan was on the back burner indefinitely.

Our differences of opinion with TNN continued with the set. We strove for a lively, 1990s look with some special effects. The network pushed for a Southwestern feel, a corral, a cowhead nailed to a gate. Jimmy Dean, who had his own network show in the 1960s, told us he was fighting the networks over stereotypical sets even then.

Music City Tonight drew fifty-five million viewers a month. There was nothing in our mail, and no research the network could give us, that indicated something was broken and needed to be fixed. Over the years TNN's own research, which was shared with us, showed our rating with the viewing audience was overwhelmingly positive. Recently those high marks were substantiated when we commissioned our own study with the highly respected television research company Frank Magid and Associates. Yet the network began soliciting ideas from other production companies on how to restructure the show. The contacts were going on before Jim Owens was asked to submit a proposal. By the time he was finally contacted, our relationship with TNN had deteriorated to the point that he declined further involvement with the network.

When there is a split in a partnership that seems to be thriving, the danger is that both parties will come off as petty when the complaints are recited. Small complaints are allowed to escalate into big ones. In the end, you must take a stand for what you believe is a principle. We did not want to compromise the show, or our reputation.

Your heart feels a wrench when you leave a job you love, in a place where you spent the last ten years. But we were flattered by the interest we received, after the announcement that we would leave TNN on or before the end of December. We appreciate the kind of item that appeared in the May 27 issue of *TV Guide*: "... we don't know if it was just a business tussle, as the official theory had it (ratings were OK), or whether it had the makings of a country song ('You take the wheels, I'll keep the truck'), but we'll miss 'em."

Our guess is that they won't have to miss us for long. The kind of quality music, news, and talk show we want to do will resurface. So, when you're channel-surfing, be looking for us. And stay tuned.

—LORIANNE CROOK
CHARLIE CHASE
July 1995

Lorianne Crook and Charlie Chase are proud to be celebrity representatives, along with Vince Gill, Reba McEntire, and Wynonna, of the Country Star Restaurants, Inc. chain of country music theme family cafés. The company's flagship restaurant, Country Star Hollywood, opened in August 1994 and is located at the entrance to the Universal Studios Hollywood® theme park in Southern California.

Country Star Restaurants are also coming soon to . . .
Atlanta • Las Vegas • New York • Orlando • London • Paris

Crook and Chase

INTERNATIONAL VIEWER CLUB

*L*orianne and Charlie invite you to be a part of their INTERNATIONAL VIEWER CLUB, which will keep you tuned in to all of the behind-the-scenes excitement and the latest Crook & Chase news. As a CROOK & CHASE INTERNATIONAL VIEWER CLUB MEMBER, you will receive:

★ 2 VIP SEATS PER MEMBERSHIP YEAR TO A CROOK & CHASE TELEVISION TAPING (subject to availability)

★ PERSONALLY AUTOGRAPHED 8" × 10" COLOR PHOTO OF CROOK & CHASE

★ LORIANNE CROOK FACT SHEET

★ CHARLIE CHASE FACT SHEET

★ "MEMBERS ONLY" COLOR PHOTO BUTTON OF CROOK & CHASE

★ QUARTERLY ISSUES OF THE CROOK AND CHASE INTERNATIONAL VIEWER CLUB NEWS

We look forward to having you as a member!

ANNUAL MEMBERSHIP FEES

U.S. Membership $12.00 (renewal $10.00)
Outside U.S. $15.00 (renewal $13.00)

Please send your U.S. check or money order along with this form to:
CROOK & CHASE INTERNATIONAL VIEWER CLUB
1525 McGavock Street
Nashville, TN 37203–3131

Please Print Clearly.

Name _____

Address _____

City _____ State _____ Zip _____

Phone (____) _____ Birth date ____/____/_____

Please allow 6 weeks for delivery.